Joshua

PURSUING THE PROMISES OF GOD
A SEEK AND FIND STUDY

NINE WEEKS IN THE BOOK OF JOSHUA

Joshua: Pursuing the Promises of God

© 2023 by Seek and Find, a collaborative group of writers advocating for Bible literacy among Christians.

ISBN: 9798373143844

All rights reserved. No part of this publication may be reproduced, stored in a retrieval system, or transmitted in any form, or by any means, except for brief quotations in printed reviews, without the prior permission of the author(s). Email summer@seekandfindstudies.com with requests.

Unless otherwise noted, all Scripture quotations are from the Christian Standard Bible®, Copyright © 2017 by Holman Bible Publishers. Used by permission. Christian Standard Bible® and CSB® are federally registered trademarks of Holman Bible Publishers.

Scripture quotations marked ESV are from the ESV® Bible (The Holy Bible, English Standard Version®), © 2001 by Crossway, a publishing ministry of Good News Publishers. Used by permission. All rights reserved.

Scripture quotations marked MEV are taken from the Modern English Version. Copyright © 2014 by Military Bible Association. Used by permission. All rights reserved.

Maps, © 2023 Joe Anderson. Used with permission.

Table of Contents

About Seek and Find Studies	4
Introduction	5
How this study works	6
How *you* work this study	7
Principles for Better Bible Study	8
Week 1: Strong and Courageous	11
Week 2: Preparing to Receive the Promise	15
Week 3: Crossing Over	31
Week 4: Faith or Judgment	47
Week 5: Leaving Nothing Undone	65
Week 6: An Unconquered Inheritance	83
Week 7: Every Promise Fulfilled	103
Week 8: A Witness Between Us	123
Week 9: Choose for Yourselves Today	139
Study Reflection	157
Supplemental Materials	158
The Family of Israel	159
Attributes of God	160
Godly Leadership	162
The Southern and Northern Campaigns Map	164
Boundaries of the Twelve Tribes Map	165

About Seek and Find Studies

Seek and Find is a collaborative group of thinkers, leaders, writers and teachers advocating for Bible literacy among Christians. We create in-depth Bible study resources for the use of the local church.

Core Characteristics of our Curriculum:
- Seek and Find studies are grounded by and rooted in the Biblical text.
- Seek and Find studies are God-centered; they train students to look first for what God says and does in every portion of Scripture.
- Seek and Find studies keep the big picture narrative of the Bible in view.
- Seek and Find studies address the interconnectedness of the Old and New Testaments.
- Seek and Find studies are diligent in highlighting the person and work of Jesus Christ.
- Seek and Find studies deal humbly and honestly with theological issues and sensitive topics by sticking closely to what can be clearly gleaned from Scripture.
- Seek and Find studies train students to recognize the Lord speaking directly and personally to them through the pages of Scripture.

More information on our studies and resources can be found at www.SeekandFindStudies.com

Acknowledgements

We are continually humbled by the minds, hearts, and talents of those who have joined us in this pursuit and are deeply thankful for their partnership.

Directors of Seek and Find
Project Managers, Lead Writers and Editors
Christi Davis and Summer Lacy

Content Development, Contribution and Review
Tyra Bevers and Suzanne Walker

Content Contributors
Lindsey Brown, Laurie Byerly, Beth Cox, Michelle Warren, Karen Watt

Review Team
Barbara Hamper, Kirstin Hancock, Barb Kassing, Jean Muñoz, Carlynn Rainey, Gillian Unruh

Creatives
Joe Anderson: Maps
Jen Kline, Line of Hope Creative: Graphic Design

Introduction

Welcome to *Pursuing the Promises of God*, a study of the book of Joshua.

The Bible is God's word to humanity. In it, He reveals who He is and the work He is doing. Each book of the Bible provides insight into specific characteristics of God.

Through Scripture, God's nature and character unfold story by story, book by book.

The book of Genesis introduces God as Creator, an almighty God of promise and covenant. In Exodus, God is Deliverer; He redeems His people from slavery and brings them to Himself. The journey through Numbers reveals God to be sovereign over the way of His people, completely worthy of trust and obedience. As we progress through the book of Joshua, we will see that God is faithful; He keeps the promises He has made to His people.

> *None of the good promises the LORD had made to the house of Israel failed.*
> *Everything was fulfilled.*
> Joshua 21:45

As the book of Joshua opens, the Israelites emerge from their years of wilderness wanderings on the outskirts of Canaan, with the entirety of God's promise before them. The land was theirs, an abundant inheritance from the Lord, but in order for the Israelites to obtain the land, they would have to go in and take it. The people could not receive the promise if they did not have the heart to pursue it.

The journey of the Israelites as they fought for the land of Canaan provides tremendous insight into the journey we take as believers today. Just as the Israelites had to learn through battle to follow, trust, and obey God in pursuit of His good promises, we who follow Christ must do the same.

Joshua is a book about a faithful God training up a faithful people. It is a book that tells of both victory and defeat, a wondrous display of God's mercy and His judgment. The book of Joshua both comforts and convicts, challenging its reader to reckon with their own resolve to pursue the promises of God. Perhaps most notably, Joshua is a book that boldly beckons followers of Christ to be strong and courageous - as we follow His lead, trust in His promises, and lay claim to our own inheritance.

For His Glory,
The Seek and Find Team

How this study works

This guide is designed to lead you through an in-depth study of the book of Joshua over the course of nine weeks. Our study of God's word is divided into three distinct parts, each specifically designed to help you dig deeper into Scripture: **Listen**, **Lean in**, and **Learn**.

Listen
First, you will "Listen" to God's voice through your individual time of study in His word, using the questions provided in this study guide. These questions teach you to implement three fundamental skills to better understand any portion of Scripture.

1. Comprehend: These questions ask you to examine what the text *says*.
2. Interpret: These questions help you discover what the text *means*.
3. Apply: These questions challenge you to recognize and respond to what the Lord is speaking to you, *personally*, through the text.

As you work your way through these questions, be watchful for the following icons:

Questions marked with ✝ draw your attention to how the text points directly to the person or work of Jesus Christ.

Questions marked with 📖 help you make connections between the Old and New Testaments.

Questions marked with ⬆ are optional; they may require additional time and study.

Lean In
After you have individually studied the assigned portion of text by answering the "Listen" questions, you will then "Lean In" to community through small group discussion. Your group leader will facilitate an exploration of what group members discovered through their independent study. A small group leader guide for this study is available for download at www.SeekAndFindStudies.com/Joshua.

Learn
Finally, after listening to God's word through independent study, and leaning into community through small group discussion, you will continue to "Learn" through a large group teaching on the text. During this session, a teacher will help you understand how everything fits together, clarify any confusion, and challenge you in your application of the material.

We highly encourage you to use teachers within your local congregations or study groups to teach this material! However, if this is not an option for your group, teachings are available at www.SeekAndFindStudies.com/Joshua.

How *you* work this study

Whether you are a brand new student of Scripture or a seasoned student of the Bible, you can use this study guide to grow deeper in your knowledge and understanding of God's word.

You will get the most out of this study by completing all three parts of the Bible study process - Listen, Lean In, and Learn - each and every week. However, the individual time you devote to the Listen portion of this guide will largely determine the amount of growth you experience.

The purpose of the Listen section is to begin building a foundational understanding of Scripture, moving from comprehension to critical thinking. The unique design of this study guide enables you to follow the process through as far as your time and knowledge of Scripture allows. If there are questions you are unable to answer, the Lean In and Learn sessions fill in any gaps.

For those of you looking for more guidance on how to structure your time, consider breaking up each week of study as follows:

Day 1: Start each week by completing the first page of that week's Listen section. This will include an intentional time of prayer, followed by reflection on what you have learned. From there, you will read through the assigned text.

Day 2: For your next day of study, work your way through the comprehension questions of the Listen section. The comprehension questions will guide you in a thorough reading of the text by training your eyes to see what the text *says*.

Days 3-4: After you finish the comprehension questions and have a thorough grasp of what the text says, you can then move confidently to the interpretation questions. These questions will push you deeper into the text as they assist you in discovering what the text *means*.

Days 5-6: Only after you have a solid understanding of what the text means, should you then move into the application section. You will conclude each week of study by considering how the Lord is prompting you to apply the truths of Scripture to your life.

Some of you will make your way through every section of study each week. Wonderful! Some of you may only be able to make it through one or two sections. Also, wonderful! Don't be discouraged by the answers you don't know or the portions of this study guide you can't complete. Instead, trust the process! The study of Scripture has a cumulative effect. Consistency is key. Understanding does not generally occur all at once, but gradually over the course of time. Even if you are unable to complete all of the questions, keep coming to the weekly meetings. By the end of this semester of study, you will have grown in your knowledge and understanding of Scripture. Most importantly, you will have grown in your relationship with the One who speaks through His word.

Principles for Better Bible Study

Keep these foundational principles in mind as you study God's word.

Principle #1: The Bible is a book about God.
The point of the Bible is God Himself. When you study the Bible, it's important to keep the point of the Bible at the center of your study. Because the Bible is a book about God, everything in the Bible points to Him. Every book, every story, every character, every event - they all reveal information regarding the nature and character of God. As you read, keep this in mind by continually asking yourself questions such as these...

What does this book, chapter, event, or character teach me about God?
How does God reveal who He is through this account?
What do I learn about God's unchanging nature through this story?

The Bible is the primary tool through which God reveals Himself to us. God-centered Bible study is one of the most powerful means through which you draw near to Him. Keeping the above questions in mind will help you keep *the point of the Bible* at the center of your study. It will help you remember that the Bible is, first and foremost, a book about God.

Principle #2: The Bible is not a book about you.
If God is the main point of the Bible, you and I are *not* the main point of the Bible. The Bible is not about us. It's about Him. However, many of us have learned to read the Bible as if it is a book about *us*. For instance, think about how often questions such as these run through your mind as you approach Bible study:

How is this information going to help me?
Improve my relationships?
Help me steward my resources?
Shape the way I make decisions?

These questions are not bad to ask, however they must not be the primary questions you ask. A good rule of thumb for Bible study is; the "He" has to come before the "me." The gospel is not about who you are, but about who He is.

You study the Bible to learn about God. Only after you comprehend what a book, verse, character or event reveals about God, can you ask yourself, "In light of what this passage reveals about God, what can I learn about myself or human nature in general?"

Principle #3: The Bible tells one big story.
The Bible tells the most amazing story of all time. The point of the entire Bible is to tell *one* story. Even though the Bible is comprised of 66 different books, written by over 40 different people during a period of over 1600 years, there is one consistent message from God to humankind. A correct understanding of the grand-scale Biblical narrative is crucial to a proper

understanding of each individual character, book, story and event in the Bible. You must study each portion of the Bible in light of the bigger story in which it is embedded. To do this, you will use the Bible to study the Bible.

Principle #4: The Bible is about real people.
The stories you read in the Bible are true stories about real people. These stories reveal information about an *actual, living* God. It is not uncommon to view the Bible as a book of fables and morality tales; a book full of principles for how to live and what kind of person one should be. This, however, is not the heart of the Bible. The heart of the Bible is that you know God through the study of His word. God chooses to reveal who He is through the stories of His people. His *real* people. Their *true* stories. As you read the Bible with this in mind, you come to see the people in the Bible are not so different from you and me; their stories bear a striking resemblance to our stories. As you come to know these real people and their stories, you better recognize God in your story.

Principle #5: The Bible is a supernatural book.
Although written by human hands, the words of the Bible are divinely inspired, with authorship of the book ultimately attributed to God Himself. Because of this, the Bible is no ordinary book and it cannot be fully understood through ordinary means. You are dependent on the Holy Spirit in your study of God's word. Use the mind God gave you to study, explore, and press into His word. Then, wholly depend on the Spirit of God to lead you to trust it, believe it, and walk in it. Be prayerful in your study of the Bible. Ask the Lord to meet you as you study and reveal Himself to you as you read; then, expect that He will!

Principle #6: Context is crucial.
The single, most important principle for studying the Bible correctly is this: Context determines everything. To understand the Bible correctly, you must seek a correct understanding of the context of the book you are studying. The Bible was written as individual books, by individual people, during certain historical times, within particular cultures, to a specific person or group of people, with a specific purpose. Understanding who wrote each book, to whom each book was written, and why it was written, will help you understand the story of the Bible as a whole (see Principle #3). When you understand the Bible as one story, in the correct context, you can then understand how it relates to you and me today.

Principle #7: Commitment is key.
Studying the Bible is a lifelong endeavor. Make a commitment to be here every week and to do the assigned reading and Listen questions. This nine week journey will require diligent effort on your part, but the payoff of studying God's word with care and consistency is rewarding! The Lord promises His living word will deeply affect our souls. Let's chase after His life-giving promises together.

Strong and Courageous

WEEK 1

Week 1: Strong and Courageous

LISTEN

Week 1 is an introductory week. There are no Listen questions for the first week of study.

LEAN IN

Begin by meeting in your small groups. Spend time getting to know one another. [1]

---

[1] Find our Small Group Leader Discussion Guide at www.SeekandFindStudies.com/Joshua

LEARN

Watch or listen to the introductory teaching session.[2] Take notes below.

---
[2] Teachings are available at www.SeekandFindStudies.com/Joshua

Preparing to Receive the Promise

WEEK 2

Week 2: Preparing to Receive the Promise

LISTEN

Pray
God is faithful; He prepares His people. Begin your time of study in prayer. Fix your mind on the faithfulness of God. Ask Him to prepare you to receive what He has promised.

> *Therefore, preparing your minds for action, and being sober-minded, set your hope fully on the grace that will be brought to you at the revelation of Jesus Christ.*
> *1 Peter 1:13 ESV*

Reflect
From the introductory session, what made the most significant impact on you?

Read with Purpose
The Bible is primarily a book about God. As you read the passage of Scripture for Week 2 (Joshua Chapters 1-2), look first for what God says and does. Using the copy of the text on the pages that follow, *highlight in blue* everything God says, and *underline in blue* everything God does.

Joshua 1-2

ENCOURAGEMENT OF JOSHUA

1 After the death of Moses the Lord's servant, the Lord spoke to Joshua son of Nun, Moses's assistant: ² "Moses my servant is dead. Now you and all the people prepare to cross over the Jordan to the land I am giving the Israelites. ³ I have given you every place where the sole of your foot treads, just as I promised Moses. ⁴ Your territory will be from the wilderness and Lebanon to the great river, the Euphrates River—all the land of the Hittites—and west to the Mediterranean Sea. ⁵ No one will be able to stand against you as long as you live. I will be with you, just as I was with Moses. I will not leave you or abandon you.

⁶ "Be strong and courageous, for you will distribute the land I swore to their ancestors to give them as an inheritance. ⁷ Above all, be strong and very courageous to observe carefully the whole instruction my servant Moses commanded you. Do not turn from it to the right or the left, so that you will have success wherever you go. ⁸ This book of instruction must not depart from your mouth; you are to meditate on it day and night so that you may carefully observe everything written in it. For then you will prosper and succeed in whatever you do. ⁹ Haven't I commanded you: be strong and courageous? Do not be afraid or discouraged, for the LORD your God is with you wherever you go."

JOSHUA PREPARES THE PEOPLE

¹⁰ Then Joshua commanded the officers of the people, ¹¹ "Go through the camp and tell the people, 'Get provisions ready for yourselves, for within three days you will be crossing the Jordan to go in and take possession of the land the LORD your God is giving you to inherit.'"

¹² Joshua said to the Reubenites, the Gadites, and half the tribe of Manasseh, ¹³ "Remember what Moses the LORD's servant commanded you when he said, 'The LORD your God will give you rest, and he will give you this land.' ¹⁴ Your wives, dependents, and livestock may remain in the land Moses gave you on this side of the Jordan. But your best soldiers must cross over in battle formation ahead of your brothers and help them ¹⁵ until the LORD gives your brothers rest, as he has given you, and they too possess the land the LORD your God is giving them. You may then return to the land of your inheritance and take possession of what Moses the LORD's servant gave you on the east side of the Jordan."

¹⁶ They answered Joshua, "Everything you have commanded us we will do, and everywhere you send us we will go. ¹⁷ We will obey you, just as we obeyed Moses in everything. Certainly the LORD your God will be with you, as he was with Moses. ¹⁸ Anyone who rebels against your order and does not obey your words in all that you command him, will be put to death. Above all, be strong and courageous!"

Week 2: Preparing to Receive the Promise

SPIES SENT TO JERICHO

2 Joshua son of Nun secretly sent two men as spies from the Acacia Grove, saying, "Go and scout the land, especially Jericho." So they left, and they came to the house of a prostitute named Rahab, and stayed there. ² The king of Jericho was told, "Look, some of the Israelite men have come here tonight to investigate the land." ³ Then the king of Jericho sent word to Rahab and said, "Bring out the men who came to you and entered your house, for they came to investigate the entire land."

⁴ But the woman had taken the two men and hidden them. So she said, "Yes, the men did come to me, but I didn't know where they were from. ⁵ At nightfall, when the city gate was about to close, the men went out, and I don't know where they were going. Chase after them quickly, and you can catch up with them!" ⁶ But she had taken them up to the roof and hidden them among the stalks of flax that she had arranged on the roof. ⁷ The men pursued them along the road to the fords of the Jordan, and as soon as they left to pursue them, the city gate was shut.

THE PROMISE TO RAHAB

⁸ Before the men fell asleep, she went up on the roof ⁹ and said to them, "I know that the LORD has given you this land and that the terror of you has fallen on us, and everyone who lives in the land is panicking because of you. ¹⁰ For we have heard how the LORD dried up the water of the Red Sea before you when you came out of Egypt, and what you did to Sihon and Og, the two Amorite kings you completely destroyed across the Jordan. ¹¹ When we heard this, we lost heart, and everyone's courage failed because of you, for the LORD your God is God in heaven above and on earth below. ¹² Now please swear to me by the LORD that you will also show kindness to my father's family, because I showed kindness to you. Give me a sure sign ¹³ that you will spare the lives of my father, mother, brothers, sisters, and all who belong to them, and save us from death."

¹⁴ The men answered her, "We will give our lives for yours. If you don't report our mission, we will show kindness and faithfulness to you when the LORD gives us the land."

¹⁵ Then she let them down by a rope through the window, since she lived in a house that was built into the wall of the city. ¹⁶ "Go to the hill country so that the men pursuing you won't find you," she said to them. "Hide there for three days until they return; afterward, go on your way."

¹⁷ The men said to her, "We will be free from this oath you made us swear, ¹⁸ unless, when we enter the land, you tie this scarlet cord to the window through which you let us down. Bring your father, mother, brothers, and all your father's family into your house. ¹⁹ If anyone goes out the doors of your house, his death will be his own fault, and we will be innocent. But if anyone with you in the house should be harmed, his death will be our fault. ²⁰ And if you report our mission, we are free from the oath you made us swear."

²¹ "Let it be as you say," she replied, and she sent them away. After they had

gone, she tied the scarlet cord to the window.
²² So the two men went into the hill country and stayed there three days until the pursuers had returned. They searched all along the way, but did not find them.
²³ Then the men returned, came down from the hill country, and crossed the Jordan. They went to Joshua son of Nun and reported everything that had happened to them. ²⁴ They told Joshua, "The LORD has handed over the entire land to us. Everyone who lives in the land is also panicking because of us."

Week 2: Preparing to Receive the Promise

Comprehend

In this section, we will examine closely what the Biblical text says. These questions are designed to help you notice and retain important details from this section of Scripture.

1. Joshua 1:1 provides important contextual information.

    a. The book of Joshua opens after the death of whom?

    b. To whom did the Lord now speak?

2. The Lord gave the people specific instructions, preparing them for what was to come.

    a. What did He tell the people to do? (1:2)

    b. What did He say He had already done? (1:3)

3. From Joshua 1:5:

    a. What did the Lord promise He *would* do?

    b. What did the Lord promise He would *not* do?

4. The Lord gave Joshua a series of instructions in Joshua 1:6-9.

List everything the Lord commanded Joshua *to do*	List everything the Lord commanded Joshua *not to* do:

5. What two things did the Lord say would result from carefully observing the instruction He had given through Moses? (1:7-8)

6. Why specifically should Joshua not be afraid or discouraged? (1:9)

7. For what reason were the people crossing the Jordan? Fill in the blanks from Joshua 1:11:

   Get provisions ready for yourselves, for within three days you will be crossing the Jordan to go in and _____ _____ _____ _____ _____ the Lord your God is giving you to inherit.

8. The nation of Israel was comprised of tribes based on the sons of Jacob. (See the *Family of Israel* visual on p.159.) As Joshua prepared the people, he provided special instructions to some of the tribes.

   a. To whom were these instructions given? (1:12)

   b. What were they instructed to do? (1:14)

   c. When could they return to their inheritance? (1:15)

   d. How did the two and a half tribes respond? (1:16-18)

9. Rahab protected the Israelite spies who had been sent to scout Jericho. From Joshua 2:8-11, summarize why.

10. What agreement did Rahab and the spies make in Joshua 2:12-14?

11. What did Rahab have to do in order for the spies to keep their oath to her? (2:17-18)

12. Upon their safe return to the Israelite camp, the spies gave Joshua a report. What did they say the Lord had done? (2:24)

13. Summarize the primary focus of this section of Scripture in a single sentence.

Week 2: Preparing to Receive the Promise

Interpret

In this section, we will be studying to discover what the text means. These questions focus your attention on specific details, draw from other parts of the Bible to improve understanding, and highlight the bigger story of Scripture.

1. Review your highlights and underlines from the Read with Purpose section.

    a. Briefly summarize the Lord's activity:

    b. What characteristics of God did you notice? You can reference the list of attributes provided on pp. 160-161 for help.

2. The book of Joshua opens with the Lord commanding Joshua to prepare the people to cross over the Jordan.

    a. Review Genesis 12:4-7. What promise of God were the people preparing to receive?

    b. This was not the Israelites' first attempt to receive this promise. Read Deuteronomy 1:21-32. What caused the previous generation to fail to receive God's promise?

3. God commanded Joshua to be "strong and courageous" and *not* to be "afraid or discouraged."

   a. Use a dictionary to define these terms:

Be	Do not be
Strong:	Afraid:
Courageous:	Discouraged:

   b. God linked two aspects of Joshua's responsibilities to the need for him to be strong and courageous. Why might strength and courage be necessary for each of the following?

   Distributing the land:

   Carefully observing the whole instruction of Moses:

4. God emphasized the importance of obedience. Read James 1:22-25 and note its message to believers.

Week 2: Preparing to Receive the Promise

5. Over the course of this study, we will learn much about godly leadership from Joshua. Answer the questions for Week 2 in the *Godly Leadership* exhibit on p. 162.

6. Joshua Chapter 2 highlights God's providence, His divine guidance over the affairs of humanity for the purpose of His sovereign will.

   a. How do we see God's providence in the spies coming to the house of Rahab?

   b. Rahab would play a much bigger role in God's sovereign plan for humanity. Read Matthew 1:1-6 and note how.

   c. What do the following passages teach about the providence of God?

   Proverbs 16:9

   Romans 8:28

23

7. Throughout Scripture, God consistently uses stories and imagery to draw our attention to the Biblical theme of salvation.

   a. Use the passages below to note specific ways in which the salvation of Rahab points to the salvation that God provided through Jesus Christ.

Rahab declared of God, "the Lord your God is God in heaven above and on earth below." (2:8)	*From Romans 10:8-13, what must humanity declare of Jesus?*
Rahab asked for the spies' kindness in sparing her and her family from death (2:12)	*Read Titus 3:4-7. How does the kindness of God spare us from death?*
Rahab asked for a "sure sign." (2:12-13)	*From Ephesians 1:13-14, what is the sure sign that Christ gives to believers?*

   b. Even the actions of the spies can bring to mind the actions of Jesus Christ. Use the table below to note similarities:

The spies were willing to save Rahab; they said, "We will give our lives for yours."	*From Galatians 1:3-4, who gave His life to save humanity?*
The spies hid three days before returning to where they were from.	*Read Matthew 12:38-40 and Mark 10:32-34. How is this similar to the experience of Jesus Christ?*

   c. The instructions given to Rahab to avoid God's judgment are similar to the instructions God gave the Israelites at Passover to avoid judgment. Read Exodus 12:21-23 and note similarities you see.

   d. In considering the salvation imagery throughout Joshua Chapter 2, what had the greatest impact on you?

Week 2: Preparing to Receive the Promise

8. In order to protect the Israelite spies, Rahab lied to the messengers of the King of Jericho.

    a. Read Hebrews 11:31 and James 2:20-26, which comment on Rahab's actions. How does Scripture characterize what she had done?

    b. This is not the first time in the Bible where someone lied to protect others from death. Read Exodus 1:15-21. How did God respond to the midwives' actions?

    c. What conclusions can believers draw from these two situations?

9. The spies made a binding oath to Rahab in the name of God. What wisdom do you see in their agreement?

10. This week, the people of God prepared to receive the promises He had made to them.

    a. What practical lessons can believers learn about preparation from Joshua and the Israelites?

    b. Just as the Israelites prepared *physically* to receive God's promises, believers are to prepare *spiritually*. What do the following passages teach about that preparation?

    1 Peter 1:13

    2 Timothy 2:21-26

25

Apply

In this section, we'll consider ways in which God is speaking to us personally. The questions to the left focus on major themes and topics from this week of study. You can use those, or anything else the Lord brought to your attention, to answer the following:

There are great promises associated with obedience to God. Has God drawn your attention to any specific area where you need to obey Him?

How have you seen the providence of God (His divine guidance) in your life?

Rahab's beliefs caused her to act. How has this challenged your faith?

God still wants His people to trust Him, to be "strong and courageous" as we follow Him. Has God brought to mind any areas where you are fearful or discouraged?

Recognize His voice:
What did the Lord draw your attention to this week?

Respond to what He has said:
How can you respond?

Week 2: Preparing to Receive the Promise

Final Thoughts
Use the space below to record any questions or takeaways you have regarding this week's material.

Repetitive Reading
It is of great benefit to repetitively read Scripture. Quickly read (or skim through) the entire book of Joshua at the end of each week of study. Record anything that stands out to you.

Pray
Think about what you have learned this week. Close by responding to the Lord in prayer.

LEAN IN

Notes from small group discussion:

LEARN

Notes from teaching session:

Crossing Over

WEEK 3

Week 3: Crossing Over

LISTEN

Pray
God is faithful; He leads His people. Spend some time thanking God for His steadfast guidance. Ask Him to increase your faith to follow as He leads.

For we walk by faith, not by sight.
2 Corinthians 5:7

Reflect
From the past week of study, what had the most significant impact on you?

Read with Purpose
The Bible is primarily a book about God. As you read the passage of Scripture for Week 3 (Joshua 3:1-5:12), look first for what God says and does. Using the copy of the text on the pages that follow, *highlight in blue* everything God says, and *underline in blue* everything God does.

Joshua 3:1–5:12

CROSSING THE JORDAN

3 Joshua started early the next morning and left the Acacia Grove with all the Israelites. They went as far as the Jordan and stayed there before crossing. ² After three days the officers went through the camp ³ and commanded the people, "When you see the ark of the covenant of the Lord your God carried by the Levitical priests, you are to break camp and follow it. ⁴ But keep a distance of about a thousand yards between yourselves and the ark. Don't go near it, so that you can see the way to go, for you haven't traveled this way before."

⁵ Joshua told the people, "Consecrate yourselves, because the LORD will do wonders among you tomorrow." ⁶ Then he said to the priests, "Carry the ark of the covenant and go on ahead of the people." So they carried the ark of the covenant and went ahead of them.

⁷ The LORD spoke to Joshua: "Today I will begin to exalt you in the sight of all Israel, so they will know that I will be with you just as I was with Moses. ⁸ Command the priests carrying the ark of the covenant: When you reach the edge of the water, stand in the Jordan."

⁹ Then Joshua told the Israelites, "Come closer and listen to the words of the LORD your God." ¹⁰ He said, "You will know that the living God is among you and that he will certainly dispossess before you the Canaanites, Hethites, Hivites, Perizzites, Girgashites, Amorites, and Jebusites ¹¹ when the ark of the covenant of the Lord of the whole earth goes ahead of you into the Jordan. ¹² Now choose twelve men from the tribes of Israel, one man for each tribe. ¹³ When the feet of the priests who carry the ark of the LORD, the Lord of the whole earth, come to rest in the Jordan's water, its water will be cut off. The water flowing downstream will stand up in a mass."

¹⁴ When the people broke camp to cross the Jordan, the priests carried the ark of the covenant ahead of the people. ¹⁵ Now the Jordan overflows its banks throughout the harvest season. But as soon as the priests carrying the ark reached the Jordan, their feet touched the water at its edge ¹⁶ and the water flowing downstream stood still, rising up in a mass that extended as far as Adam, a city next to Zarethan. The water flowing downstream into the Sea of the Arabah—the Dead Sea—was completely cut off, and the people crossed opposite Jericho. ¹⁷ The priests carrying the ark of the LORD's covenant stood firmly on dry ground in the middle of the Jordan, while all Israel crossed on dry ground until the entire nation had finished crossing the Jordan.

THE MEMORIAL STONES

4 After the entire nation had finished crossing the Jordan, the LORD spoke to Joshua: ² "Choose twelve men from the people, one man for each tribe, ³ and command them: Take twelve stones from this place in the middle of the Jordan where the priests are standing, carry them with you, and set them down at the place where you spend the night."

⁴ So Joshua summoned the twelve men he had selected from the Israelites, one man for each tribe, ⁵ and said to them, "Go across to the ark of the LORD your God in the middle of the Jordan. Each of you lift a stone onto his shoulder, one for each of the Israelite tribes, ⁶ so that this will be a sign among you. In the future, when your children ask you, 'What do these stones mean to you?' ⁷ you should tell them, 'The water of the Jordan was cut off in front of the ark of the LORD's covenant. When it crossed the Jordan, the Jordan's water was cut off.' Therefore these stones will always be a memorial for the Israelites." ⁸ The Israelites did just as Joshua had commanded them. The twelve men took stones from the middle of the Jordan, one for each of the Israelite tribes, just as the LORD had told Joshua. They carried them to the camp and set them down there. ⁹ Joshua also set up twelve stones in the middle of the Jordan where the priests who carried the ark of the covenant were standing. The stones are still there today.

¹⁰ The priests carrying the ark continued standing in the middle of the Jordan until everything was completed that the LORD had commanded Joshua to tell the people, in keeping with all that Moses had commanded Joshua. The people hurried across, ¹¹ and after everyone had finished crossing, the priests with the ark of the LORD crossed in the sight of the people. ¹² The Reubenites, Gadites, and half the tribe of Manasseh went in battle formation in front of the Israelites, as Moses had instructed them. ¹³ About forty thousand equipped for war crossed to the plains of Jericho in the LORD's presence.

¹⁴ On that day the LORD exalted Joshua in the sight of all Israel, and they revered him throughout his life, as they had revered Moses. ¹⁵ The LORD told Joshua, ¹⁶ "Command the priests who carry the ark of the testimony to come up from the Jordan."

¹⁷ So Joshua commanded the priests, "Come up from the Jordan." ¹⁸ When the priests carrying the ark of the LORD's covenant came up from the middle of the Jordan, and their feet stepped out on solid ground, the water of the Jordan resumed its course, flowing over all the banks as before.

¹⁹ The people came up from the Jordan on the tenth day of the first month, and camped at Gilgal on the eastern limits of Jericho. ²⁰ Then Joshua set up in Gilgal the twelve stones they had taken from the Jordan, ²¹ and he said to the Israelites, "In the future, when your children ask their fathers, 'What is the meaning of these stones?' ²² you should tell your children, 'Israel crossed the Jordan on dry ground.' ²³ For the LORD your God dried up the water of the Jordan before you until you had crossed over, just as the LORD your God did to the Red Sea, which he dried up before us until we had crossed over. ²⁴ This is so that all the peoples of the earth may know that the LORD's hand is strong, and so that you may always fear the LORD your God."

CIRCUMCISION OF THE ISRAELITES

5 When all the Amorite kings across the Jordan to the west and all the Canaanite kings near the sea heard how the LORD had dried up the water of the Jordan before the Israelites until they had crossed over, they lost heart and their courage failed because of the Israelites.

² At that time the LORD said to Joshua, "Make flint knives and circumcise the Israelite men again." ³ So Joshua made flint knives and circumcised the Israelite men at Gibeath-haaraloth. ⁴ This is the reason Joshua circumcised them: All the people who came out of Egypt who were males—all the men of war—had died in the wilderness along the way after they had come out of Egypt. ⁵ Though all the people who came out were circumcised, none of the people born in the wilderness along the way were circumcised after they had come out of Egypt. ⁶ For the Israelites wandered in the wilderness forty years until all the nation's men of war who came out of Egypt had died off because they did not obey the LORD. So the LORD vowed never to let them see the land he had sworn to their ancestors to give us, a land flowing with milk and honey. ⁷ He raised up their sons in their place; it was these Joshua circumcised. They were still uncircumcised, since they had not been circumcised along the way. ⁸ After the entire nation had been circumcised, they stayed where they were in the camp until they recovered. ⁹ The LORD then said to Joshua, "Today I have rolled away the disgrace of Egypt from you." Therefore, that place is still called Gilgal today.

FOOD FROM THE LAND

¹⁰ While the Israelites camped at Gilgal on the plains of Jericho, they observed the Passover on the evening of the fourteenth day of the month. ¹¹ The day after Passover they ate unleavened bread and roasted grain from the produce of the land. ¹² And the day after they ate from the produce of the land, the manna ceased. Since there was no more manna for the Israelites, they ate from the crops of the land of Canaan that year.

Week 3: Crossing Over

Comprehend

In this section, we will examine closely what the Biblical text says. These questions are designed to help you notice and retain important details from this section of Scripture.

1. Early the next morning, Joshua and the Israelites set out for the Jordan River. What were they to follow when they crossed it? (3:3)

2. Joshua commanded the Israelites to consecrate themselves. Why were they to do this? (3:5)

3. The Lord spoke to Joshua in Joshua 3:7-8.

    a. What did the Lord tell Joshua He was going to do?

    b. Why would He do this?

4. From Joshua 3:10, what two things would the Israelites know when the ark of the covenant went ahead of them into the Jordan?

5. The Lord commanded the priests carrying the ark to stand in the Jordan.

    a. What happened as soon as their feet touched the water? (3:15-16)

    b. Who crossed on dry ground? (3:17)

6. In Joshua Chapter 4, God commanded Joshua to have the Israelites take twelve stones from the middle of the Jordan.

    a. Where were these stones to be placed? (4:8, 20)

    b. What purpose would these stones serve? (4:6-7)

7. Joshua had a second set of 12 stones set up as well. Where were these stones placed? (4:9)

8. How many soldiers crossed onto the plains of Jericho that day? (4:13)

9. Use Joshua 4:14 to fill in the blanks below:

   On that day the Lord _____ _____ in the sight of all Israel, and they revered him throughout his life, as they had revered Moses.

10. What happened when the priest carrying the ark of the Lord's covenant stepped out of the Jordan and onto solid ground? (4:18)

11. God's miracle at the Jordan accomplished at least two things according to Joshua 4:24.

    a. What would all the people of the earth know as a result of this miracle?

    b. What would the result be for God's people?

12. How were the Amorite and Canaanite kings impacted by what the Lord had done? (5:1)

13. What did the Lord tell Joshua to do in Joshua 5:2?

14. Fill in the blanks with the Lord's words to Joshua after the entire nation was circumcised (5:9):

    Today I have rolled away the _____ of _____ from you.

15. What did the people observe while camped at Gilgal? (5:10)

16. What ceased the day after the Israelites ate from the produce of the land? (5:12)

17. Summarize the primary focus of this section of Scripture in a single sentence.

Week 3: Crossing Over

Interpret

In this section, we will be studying to discover what the text means. These questions focus your attention on specific details, draw from other parts of the Bible to improve understanding, and highlight the bigger story of Scripture.

1. Review your highlights and underlines from the Read with Purpose section.

    a. Briefly summarize the Lord's activity:

    b. What characteristics of God did you notice? You can reference the list of attributes provided on pp. 160-161 for help.

2. Before crossing the Jordan, the people were to be consecrated, formally dedicated to a divine purpose. Read Numbers 33:50-53. What divine purpose were the Israelites to fulfill?

3. God wanted the people to know that He would be the one to dispossess the inhabitants of the land so that the Israelites could inherit it.

    a. Read Psalm 24:1. What right does God have to take land from one people group and give it to another?

    b. Now read Deuteronomy 9:1-6 and fill in the table below:

Why was the Lord going to drive out these nations?	
Why was God giving the land to the Israelites?	
What did Moses warn them not to think regarding why God was giving them the land?	

4. The Israelites' crossing of the Jordan River into Canaan bears a striking resemblance to their crossing of the Red Sea out of Egypt.

   a. Compare Joshua 3:15-4:17 to Exodus 14:15-31. Make note of similarities and differences between these two miraculous events.

Similarities	Differences

   b. What stands out to you most from comparing these events?

5. This week, we were told that the miracle of the Jordan crossing would cause the people to "always fear the Lord." What do the following passages teach about the fear of the Lord?

   Proverbs 9:10

   Exodus 20:20

   Deuteronomy 6:24

Week 3: Crossing Over

6. In Joshua Chapter 5, we encountered several topics of profound significance to Israel's relationship with God.

    a. Use the table below to note important information about each topic:

Topic	Passage	Question(s)
Circumcision	Genesis 17:1-11	Circumcision was a sign of what?
Passover	Exodus 12:21-27 Exodus 12:48-49	What did Passover commemorate and how was it related to circumcision?
Unleavened Bread	Exodus 12:14-17	Why did they eat unleavened bread?
Manna	Exodus 16:31-35	What was the manna?

    b. These topics *still* have profound significance to believers' relationship with God. Look up the passages below and note what you learn.

Topic	Passage	Question(s)
Circumcision	Romans 2:28-29 Galatians 6:15 Philippians 3:3	What is true circumcision?
Passover	John 1:29	Who is the true Passover lamb and what has He done?
Unleavened Bread	1 Corinthians 5:6-8	What does unleavened bread symbolize?
Manna	John 6:29-35	Who is the true bread from heaven (manna) and what has He done?

    c. What impacts you the most after closely considering these topics in both their Old and New Testament contexts?

39

7. There are many parallels between God's supernatural provision for the Israelites' *exodus* from their slavery in Egypt and His supernatural provision for their *entrance* into the Promised Land.

    a. Consider some of these parallels as provided in the chart below:

Parallels	Exodus from slavery in Egypt	Entrance into the Promised Land
Events happening on the 10th day of the first month	The Passover lamb was selected. (Exodus 12:1-6)	The people came up from the Jordan. (Joshua 4:17-19)
Events happening on the 14th day of the first month (Passover)	The people applied the blood of the Passover lamb to their doorposts and were spared God's judgment. (Exodus 12:5-13, 21-23)	The Israelites observed the holiday of Passover by the Jordan. (Joshua 5:10)
Events happening during the Festival of Unleavened Bread	God brought the Israelites out of the land of Egypt. (Exodus 12:14-20)	The Israelites entered Canaan; they ate unleavened bread and the produce of the land. The manna ceased. (Joshua 5:10-12)
Emphasis on Memorial	Right after the Passover, commands were given regarding remembrance. (Exodus 12:14, 13:6-10)	Right after crossing the Jordan, commands were given regarding remembrance. (Joshua 4:1-9)
Need for Circumcision	God commanded circumcision for anyone who wanted to celebrate Passover. (Exodus 12:43-49)	God commanded circumcision for the people born in the wilderness who hadn't been circumcised. (Joshua 5:2-8)
Need for Consecration	After the Passover, God commanded all firstborn sons to be consecrated to Him. (Exodus 13:1)	Before crossing the Jordan, Joshua had all the people consecrate themselves. (Joshua 3:5)
People equipped for battle	The people left Egypt equipped for battle. (Exodus 13:18)	The people crossed the Jordan equipped for battle. (Joshua 4:13)
People cross a body of water on dry ground	The people crossed the Red Sea on dry ground. (Exodus 14:15-22)	The people crossed the Jordan on dry ground. (Joshua 3:17)

    b. What takeaways do you have from considering the parallels between these two events?

Week 3: Crossing Over

8. God's supernatural provision for both the Israelites' *exodus* from slavery in Egypt and their *entrance* into the Promised Land points to the greater provision He would make for believers.

   a. From Romans 6:6-11, how has God provided for a believer's exodus from slavery to sin?

   b. According to John 3:16, how has God provided for a believer's entrance into eternal life?

9. Joshua demonstrated godly leadership as the Israelites crossed into the Promised Land. Fill in the *Godly Leadership* exhibit on p. 163 with information from this week's text.

10. This week, the people of God stepped out in faith and crossed over into the land the Lord was giving them.

    a. What practical lessons can believers learn about faith from Joshua and the Israelites?

    b. The Israelites stepped out in faith in order to receive God's promises, and believers must do the same. Read the following passages and note what they teach about faith.

    Hebrews 11:6

    Romans 1:17

    1 Corinthians 2:4-5

Apply

In this section, we'll consider ways in which God is speaking to us personally. The questions to the left focus on major themes and topics from this week of study. You can use those, or anything else the Lord brought to your attention, to answer the following:

How have you seen God move as you have stepped out in faith?

Memorials provide opportunities for us to share what the Lord has done. What memorials do you sense God is leading you to establish?

How has God expanded or challenged your understanding of faith?

God removed from Israel the disgrace of Egypt in one day! Has He done the same for you? How?

Obedience to the LORD is essential. Has God drawn your attention to any area where you should focus on obedience?

Recognize His voice:
What did the Lord draw your attention to this week?

Respond to what He has said:
How can you respond?

Week 3: Crossing Over

Final Thoughts
Use the space below to record any questions or takeaways you have regarding this week's material.

Repetitive Reading
It is of great benefit to repetitively read Scripture. Quickly read (or skim through) the entire book of Joshua at the end of each week of study. Record anything that stands out to you.

Pray
Think about what you have learned this week. Close by responding to the Lord in prayer.

LEAN IN

Notes from small group discussion:

Week 3: Crossing Over

LEARN

Notes from teaching session:

Faith or Judgment

WEEK 4

Week 4: Faith or Judgment

LISTEN

Pray
God is faithful; He does what He says He will do. Begin your time of study in prayer. Thank God that His word can be trusted. Ask Him to help you more fully believe His promises and heed His warnings.

> *The Rock–his work is perfect; all his ways are just. A faithful God, without bias, he is righteous and true.*
> Deuteronomy 32:4

Reflect
From the past week of study, what had the most significant impact on you?

Read with Purpose
The Bible is primarily a book about God. As you read the passage of Scripture for Week 4 (Joshua 5:13-8:35), look first for what God says and does. Using the copy of the text on the pages that follow, *highlight in blue* everything God says, and *underline in blue* everything God does.

Joshua 5:13–8:35

COMMANDER OF THE LORD'S ARMY

5 ¹³ When Joshua was near Jericho, he looked up and saw a man standing in front of him with a drawn sword in his hand. Joshua approached him and asked, "Are you for us or for our enemies?"

¹⁴ "Neither," he replied. "I have now come as commander of the LORD's army." Then Joshua bowed with his face to the ground in homage and asked him, "What does my lord want to say to his servant?"

¹⁵ The commander of the LORD's army said to Joshua, "Remove the sandals from your feet, for the place where you are standing is holy." And Joshua did that.

THE CONQUEST OF JERICHO

6 Now Jericho was strongly fortified because of the Israelites—no one leaving or entering. ² The LORD said to Joshua, "Look, I have handed Jericho, its king, and its best soldiers over to you. ³ March around the city with all the men of war, circling the city one time. Do this for six days. ⁴ Have seven priests carry seven ram's-horn trumpets in front of the ark. But on the seventh day, march around the city seven times, while the priests blow the rams' horns. ⁵ When there is a prolonged blast of the horn and you hear its sound, have all the troops give a mighty shout. Then the city wall will collapse, and the troops will advance, each man straight ahead."

⁶ So Joshua son of Nun summoned the priests and said to them, "Take up the ark of the covenant and have seven priests carry seven rams' horns in front of the ark of the LORD." ⁷ He said to the troops, "Move forward, march around the city, and have the armed men go ahead of the ark of the LORD."

⁸ After Joshua had spoken to the troops, seven priests carrying seven rams' horns before the LORD moved forward and blew the rams' horns; the ark of the LORD's covenant followed them.

⁹ While the rams' horns were blowing, the armed men went in front of the priests who blew the rams' horns, and the rear guard went behind the ark.

¹⁰ But Joshua had commanded the troops, "Do not shout or let your voice be heard. Don't let one word come out of your mouth until the time I say, 'Shout!' Then you are to shout." ¹¹ So the ark of the LORD was carried around the city, circling it once. They returned to the camp and spent the night there.

¹² Joshua got up early the next morning. The priests took the ark of the LORD, ¹³ and the seven priests carrying seven rams' horns marched in front of the ark of the LORD. While the rams' horns were blowing, the armed men went in front of them, and the rear guard went behind the ark of the LORD. ¹⁴ On the second day they marched around the city once and returned to the camp. They did this for six days.

¹⁵ Early on the seventh day, they started at dawn and marched around the city seven times in the same way. That was the only day they marched around the city seven times. ¹⁶ After the seventh time, the priests blew the rams' horns, and

Joshua said to the troops, "Shout! For the LORD has given you the city. [17] But the city and everything in it are set apart to the LORD for destruction. Only Rahab the prostitute and everyone with her in the house will live, because she hid the messengers we sent. [18] But keep yourselves from the things set apart, or you will be set apart for destruction. If you take any of those things, you will set apart the camp of Israel for destruction and make trouble for it. [19] For all the silver and gold, and the articles of bronze and iron, are dedicated to the LORD and must go into the LORD's treasury."

[20] So the troops shouted, and the rams' horns sounded. When they heard the blast of the ram's horn, the troops gave a great shout, and the wall collapsed. The troops advanced into the city, each man straight ahead, and they captured the city. [21] They completely destroyed everything in the city with the sword—every man and woman, both young and old, and every ox, sheep, and donkey.

RAHAB AND HER FAMILY SPARED

[22] Joshua said to the two men who had scouted the land, "Go to the prostitute's house and bring the woman out of there, and all who are with her, just as you swore to her." [23] So the young men who had scouted went in and brought out Rahab and her father, mother, brothers, and all who belonged to her. They brought out her whole family and settled them outside the camp of Israel.

[24] They burned the city and everything in it, but they put the silver and gold and the articles of bronze and iron into the treasury of the LORD's house.

[25] However, Joshua spared Rahab the prostitute, her father's family, and all who belonged to her, because she hid the messengers Joshua had sent to spy on Jericho, and she still lives in Israel today.

[26] At that time Joshua imposed this curse:
The man who undertakes
the rebuilding of this city, Jericho,
is cursed before the LORD.
He will lay its foundation
at the cost of his firstborn;
he will finish its gates
at the cost of his youngest.

[27] And the LORD was with Joshua, and his fame spread throughout the land.

DEFEAT AT AI

7 The Israelites, however, were unfaithful regarding the things set apart for destruction. Achan son of Carmi, son of Zabdi, son of Zerah, of the tribe of Judah, took some of what was set apart, and the LORD's anger burned against the Israelites.

[2] Joshua sent men from Jericho to Ai, which is near Beth-aven, east of Bethel, and told them, "Go up and scout the land." So the men went up and scouted Ai.

[3] After returning to Joshua they reported to him, "Don't send all the people,

but send about two thousand or three thousand men to attack Ai. Since the people of Ai are so few, don't wear out all our people there." ⁴ So about three thousand men went up there, but they fled from the men of Ai. ⁵ The men of Ai struck down about thirty-six of them and chased them from outside the city gate to the quarries, striking them down on the descent. As a result, the people lost heart.

⁶ Then Joshua tore his clothes and fell facedown to the ground before the ark of the LORD until evening, as did the elders of Israel; they all put dust on their heads. ⁷ "Oh, LORD God," Joshua said, "why did you ever bring these people across the Jordan to hand us over to the Amorites for our destruction? If only we had been content to remain on the other side of the Jordan!

⁸ What can I say, Lord, now that Israel has turned its back and run from its enemies? ⁹ When the Canaanites and all who live in the land hear about this, they will surround us and wipe out our name from the earth. Then what will you do about your great name?"

¹⁰ The LORD then said to Joshua, "Stand up! Why have you fallen facedown? ¹¹ Israel has sinned. They have violated my covenant that I appointed for them. They have taken some of what was set apart. They have stolen, deceived, and put those things with their own belongings. ¹² This is why the Israelites cannot stand against their enemies. They will turn their backs and run from their enemies, because they have been set apart for destruction. I will no longer be with you unless you remove from among you what is set apart.

¹³ "Go and consecrate the people. Tell them to consecrate themselves for tomorrow, for this is what the LORD, the God of Israel, says: There are things that are set apart among you, Israel. You will not be able to stand against your enemies until you remove what is set apart. ¹⁴ In the morning, present yourselves tribe by tribe. The tribe the LORD selects is to come forward clan by clan. The clan the LORD selects is to come forward family by family. The family the LORD selects is to come forward man by man. ¹⁵ The one who is caught with the things set apart must be burned, along with everything he has, because he has violated the LORD's covenant and committed an outrage in Israel."

ACHAN JUDGED

¹⁶ Joshua got up early the next morning. He had Israel come forward tribe by tribe, and the tribe of Judah was selected. ¹⁷ He had the clans of Judah come forward, and the Zerahite clan was selected. He had the Zerahite clan come forward by heads of families, and Zabdi was selected. ¹⁸ He then had Zabdi's family come forward man by man, and Achan son of Carmi, son of Zabdi, son of Zerah, of the tribe of Judah, was selected.

¹⁹ So Joshua said to Achan, "My son, give glory to the LORD, the God of Israel, and make a confession to him. I urge you, tell me what you have done. Don't hide anything from me."

²⁰ Achan replied to Joshua, "It is true. I have sinned against the LORD, the God of Israel. This is what I did: ²¹ When I saw among the spoils a beautiful cloak

from Babylon, five pounds of silver, and a bar of gold weighing a pound and a quarter, I coveted them and took them. You can see for yourself. They are concealed in the ground inside my tent, with the silver under the cloak." ²² So Joshua sent messengers who ran to the tent, and there was the cloak, concealed in his tent, with the silver underneath. ²³ They took the things from inside the tent, brought them to Joshua and all the Israelites, and spread them out in the LORD's presence.

²⁴ Then Joshua and all Israel with him took Achan son of Zerah, the silver, the cloak, and the bar of gold, his sons and daughters, his ox, donkey, and sheep, his tent, and all that he had, and brought them up to the Valley of Achor. ²⁵ Joshua said, "Why have you brought us trouble? Today the LORD will bring you trouble!" So all Israel stoned them to death. They burned their bodies, threw stones on them, ²⁶ and raised over him a large pile of rocks that remains still today. Then the LORD turned from his burning anger. Therefore that place is called the Valley of Achor still today.

CONQUEST OF AI

8 The LORD said to Joshua, "Do not be afraid or discouraged. Take all the troops with you and go attack Ai. Look, I have handed over to you the king of Ai, his people, city, and land. ² Treat Ai and its king as you did Jericho and its king, except that you may plunder its spoil and livestock for yourselves. Set an ambush behind the city."

³ So Joshua and all the troops set out to attack Ai. Joshua selected thirty thousand of his best soldiers and sent them out at night. ⁴ He commanded them, "Pay attention. Lie in ambush behind the city, not too far from it, and all of you be ready. ⁵ Then I and all the people who are with me will approach the city. When they come out against us as they did the first time, we will flee from them. ⁶ They will come after us until we have drawn them away from the city, for they will say, 'They are fleeing from us as before.' While we are fleeing from them, ⁷ you are to come out of your ambush and seize the city. The LORD your God will hand it over to you. ⁸ After taking the city, set it on fire. Follow the LORD's command—see that you do as I have ordered you." ⁹ So Joshua sent them out, and they went to the ambush site and waited between Bethel and Ai, to the west of Ai. But he spent that night with the troops.

¹⁰ Joshua started early the next morning and mobilized them. Then he and the elders of Israel led the people up to Ai. ¹¹ All the troops who were with him went up and approached the city, arriving opposite Ai, and camped to the north of it, with a valley between them and the city. ¹² Now Joshua had taken about five thousand men and set them in ambush between Bethel and Ai, to the west of the city. ¹³ The troops were stationed in this way: the main camp to the north of the city and its rear guard to the west of the city. And that night Joshua went into the valley.

¹⁴ When the king of Ai saw the Israelites, the men of the city hurried and went out early in the morning so that he and all his people could engage Israel in battle at a suitable place facing the Arabah. But he did not know there was an

ambush waiting for him behind the city. ¹⁵ Joshua and all Israel pretended to be beaten back by them and fled toward the wilderness. ¹⁶ Then all the troops of Ai were summoned to pursue them, and they pursued Joshua and were drawn away from the city. ¹⁷ Not a man was left in Ai or Bethel who did not go out after Israel, leaving the city exposed while they pursued Israel.

¹⁸ Then the LORD said to Joshua, "Hold out the javelin in your hand toward Ai, for I will hand the city over to you." So Joshua held out his javelin toward it. ¹⁹ When he held out his hand, the men in ambush rose quickly from their position. They ran, entered the city, captured it, and immediately set it on fire. ²⁰ The men of Ai turned and looked back, and smoke from the city was rising to the sky! They could not escape in any direction, and the troops who had fled to the wilderness now became the pursuers. ²¹ When Joshua and all Israel saw that the men in ambush had captured the city and that smoke was rising from it, they turned back and struck down the men of Ai. ²² Then men in ambush came out of the city against them, and the men of Ai were trapped between the Israelite forces, some on one side and some on the other. They struck them down until no survivor or fugitive remained, ²³ but they captured the king of Ai alive and brought him to Joshua.

²⁴ When Israel had finished killing everyone living in Ai who had pursued them into the open country, and when every last one of them had fallen by the sword, all Israel returned to Ai and struck it down with the sword. ²⁵ The total of those who fell that day, both men and women, was twelve thousand—all the people of Ai. ²⁶ Joshua did not draw back his hand that was holding the javelin until all the inhabitants of Ai were completely destroyed. ²⁷ Israel plundered only the cattle and spoil of that city for themselves, according to the LORD's command that he had given Joshua.

²⁸ Joshua burned Ai and left it a permanent ruin, still desolate today. ²⁹ He hung the body of the king of Ai on a tree until evening, and at sunset Joshua commanded that they take his body down from the tree. They threw it down at the entrance of the city gate and put a large pile of rocks over it, which still remains today.

RENEWED COMMITMENT TO THE LAW

³⁰ At that time Joshua built an altar on Mount Ebal to the LORD, the God of Israel, ³¹ just as Moses the LORD's servant had commanded the Israelites. He built it according to what is written in the book of the law of Moses: an altar of uncut stones on which no iron tool has been used. Then they offered burnt offerings to the LORD and sacrificed fellowship offerings on it. ³² There on the stones, Joshua copied the law of Moses, which he had written in the presence of the Israelites. ³³ All Israel—resident alien and citizen alike—with their elders, officers, and judges, stood on either side of the ark of the LORD's covenant facing the Levitical priests who carried it. Half of them were in front of Mount Gerizim and half in front of Mount Ebal, as Moses the LORD's servant had commanded earlier concerning blessing the people of Israel. ³⁴ Afterward, Joshua read aloud all the words of the law—the blessings as well as the curses—

according to all that is written in the book of the law. ³⁵ There was not a word of all that Moses had commanded that Joshua did not read before the entire assembly of Israel, including the women, the dependents, and the resident aliens who lived among them.

Comprehend

In this section, we will examine closely what the Biblical text says. These questions are designed to help you notice and retain important details from this section of Scripture.

1. When Joshua was near Jericho, he encountered a man "with a drawn sword in his hand."

    a. What question did Joshua ask him? (5:13)

    b. How did he respond? (5:14)

2. As Joshua Chapter 6 begins, what was the state of Jericho and why?

3. According to Joshua 6:2, what did the Lord say He had already done?

4. Summarize the instructions given to the troops for each of the following days:

    Days 1-6 (6:3-4)

    Day 7 (6:4-5)

5. What would happen when these actions were completed? (6:5)

6. The Israelites were given a warning concerning the things set apart. What would happen if they disobeyed: To them, personally? To the camp of Israel as a whole? (6:18)

7. What became of Rahab and her family? (6:23-25)

8. Fill in the blanks from Joshua 6:27:

    And the LORD was with Joshua, and his fame spread _____ the land.

Week 4: Faith or Judgment

9. Joshua 7:1 tells us that the Israelites "were unfaithful regarding the things set apart for destruction."

    a. What had happened? (7:1)

    b. What was the result? (7:1)

10. Next, Joshua commanded an unsuccessful attack against the city of Ai.

    a. How many men were struck down? (7:5)

    b. What impact did this have on the people? (7:5)

    c. How did Joshua respond? (7:6-9)

11. Look closely at the Lord's response to Joshua. List everything you see regarding the following: (7:10-12)

What had the Israelites done?	What would be the result?

12. What would the people have to do in order to once again stand against their enemies? (7:13)

13. What was to be done to the one caught with the things set apart for destruction and why? (7:15)

14. What reassurance did the Lord provide Joshua regarding Ai in Joshua 8:1?

15. How did Joshua and the Israelites respond to the Lord after their victory at Ai? List everything you see. (8:30-35)

16. Summarize the primary focus of this section of Scripture in a single sentence.

Interpret

In this section, we will be studying to discover what the text means. These questions focus your attention on specific details, draw from other parts of the Bible to improve understanding, and highlight the bigger story of Scripture.

1. Review your highlights and underlines from the Read with Purpose section.

    a. Briefly summarize the Lord's activity:

    b. What characteristics of God did you notice? You can reference the list of attributes provided on pp. 160-161 for help.

2. Joshua's encounter with the commander of the Lord's army bears a striking resemblance to Moses' encounter at the burning bush. Compare Exodus 3:1-12 and Joshua 5:13-6:5.

    a. What similarities do you see between these two encounters?

    b. God's timing is purposeful. Consider the likely impact these encounters would have had on these men. Make notes below.

Impact on Moses	Impact on Joshua

Week 4: Faith or Judgment

3. The Israelites' entrance to the Promised Land at Jericho was the fulfillment of one of God's great promises to them, and it was announced by trumpets and a loud shout. Read 1 Thessalonians 4:16-17. What future promise of God will be announced in the same way?

4. The Israelites' entrance to the Promised Land was the fulfillment of one of God's great promises to them. This same event, however, meant judgment for the inhabitants of the land.

    a. Read the following passages and note what they teach about God's judgment.

    Psalm 9:8

    Jeremiah 17:10

    Ezekiel 18:30-32

    John 3:16-21

    b. Just as the Israelites' entrance to the Promised Land meant judgment for the Canaanites, Christ's return will mean judgment for all who have not accepted salvation through Jesus Christ. Read 2 Peter 3:1-13 and summarize its message below.

5. Achan's sin brought God's wrath on the entire community. In an effort to turn His wrath away, Israel stoned Achan and his entire family.

    a. What evidence do you see from this week's passage that might indicate that God approved of this action?

    b. Read Deuteronomy 24:16 and Ezekiel 18:20. How do these passages impact your thinking?

6. During Israel's second attack on Ai, God told Joshua to hold out his javelin. This account is similar to an earlier event in Joshua's life.

    a. Read Exodus 17:8-16. What stands out to you from these two accounts?

    b. How might this have bolstered Joshua's faith?

7. What lessons can believers learn from the conquest of Ai? Consider everything from the initial attack, their defeat, their reaction to their defeat, the second attack, etc.

8. In Joshua 8:30-35, Joshua performed the ceremony commanded in Deuteronomy Chapters 27-28.

    a. Consider the timing. Why might Joshua choose to do this at this time?

    b. What do you think would be the desired outcome of this action?

Week 4: Faith or Judgment

9. Joshua's faith was tested and proven through both the victories Israel won and the defeats they suffered. Fill in the *Godly Leadership* exhibit on p. 163 with information from this week's study.

10. This week's passage highlights two extremes: faith, which leads to victory, and unbelief, which leads to judgment.

   a. Hebrews 11:30-31 tells us that the Israelites marching around Jericho and Rahab's actions demonstrated faith. What other instances of faith do you see from this week's passage?

   b. The opposite of faith is unbelief. From this week's passage, what did unbelief look like in the inhabitants of Canaan? In God's people?

   c. Read James 2:14-26 and note what it teaches about true faith.

> *By faith the walls of Jericho fell down after being marched around by the Israelites for seven days. By faith Rahab the prostitute welcomed the spies in peace and didn't perish with those who disobeyed. Hebrews 11:30-31*

Apply

In this section, we'll consider ways in which God is speaking to us personally. The questions to the left focus on major themes and topics from this week of study. You can use those, or anything else the Lord brought to your attention, to answer the following:

God gave powerful experiences to Moses and Joshua at key times. What powerful experiences has He provided for you? How have they impacted your faith?

Faith is believing both God's promises and His warnings. Has God drawn your attention to any area where you need to believe Him now?

When faced with defeat, Joshua and the leaders' initial reaction was to think God had abandoned them instead of considering if they had done something wrong. Are you prone to do the same?

Recognize His voice:
What did the Lord draw your attention to this week?

Respond to what He has said:
How can you respond?

Week 4: Faith or Judgment

Final Thoughts
Use the space below to record any questions or takeaways you have regarding this week's material.

Repetitive Reading
It is of great benefit to repetitively read Scripture. Quickly read (or skim through) the entire book of Joshua at the end of each week of study. Record anything that stands out to you.

Pray
Think about what you have learned this week. Close by responding to the Lord in prayer.

LEAN IN

Notes from small group discussion:

Week 4: Faith or Judgment

LEARN

Notes from teaching session:

Leaving Nothing Undone

WEEK 5

Week 5: Leaving Nothing Undone

LISTEN

Pray
God is faithful; He is the one who provides victory in battle. Begin your time of study in prayer. Ask God to impress upon you the importance of following His lead in the battles you face. Ask Him to help you leave nothing undone.

> *This is what the Lord says: 'Do not be afraid or discouraged because of this vast number, for the battle is not yours, but God's.*
> *2 Chronicles 20:15*

Reflect
From the past week of study, what had the most significant impact on you?

Read with Purpose
The Bible is primarily a book about God. As you read the passage of Scripture for Week 5 (Joshua Chapters 9-12), look first for what God says and does. Using the copy of the text on the pages that follow, *highlight in blue* everything God says, and *underline in blue* everything God does.

Note: This week's passage is fairly long. Your aim for Read with Purpose should be to read the text quickly, preferably in one sitting.

Joshua 9-12

DECEPTION BY GIBEON

9 When all the kings heard about Jericho and Ai, those who were west of the Jordan in the hill country, in the Judean foothills, and all along the coast of the Mediterranean Sea toward Lebanon—the Hethites, Amorites, Canaanites, Perizzites, Hivites, and Jebusites— ² they formed a unified alliance to fight against Joshua and Israel.

³ When the inhabitants of Gibeon heard what Joshua had done to Jericho and Ai, ⁴ they acted deceptively. They gathered provisions and took worn-out sacks on their donkeys and old wineskins, cracked and mended. ⁵ They wore old, patched sandals on their feet and threadbare clothing on their bodies. Their entire provision of bread was dry and crumbly. ⁶ They went to Joshua in the camp at Gilgal and said to him and the men of Israel, "We have come from a distant land. Please make a treaty with us."

⁷ The men of Israel replied to the Hivites, "Perhaps you live among us. How can we make a treaty with you?"

⁸ They said to Joshua, "We are your servants."

Then Joshua asked them, "Who are you and where do you come from?"

⁹ They replied to him, "Your servants have come from a faraway land because of the reputation of the LORD your God. For we have heard of his fame, and all that he did in Egypt, ¹⁰ and all that he did to the two Amorite kings beyond the Jordan—King Sihon of Heshbon and King Og of Bashan, who was in Ashtaroth. ¹¹ So our elders and all the inhabitants of our land told us, 'Take provisions with you for the journey; go and meet them and say, "We are your servants. Please make a treaty with us."' ¹² This bread of ours was warm when we took it from our houses as food on the day we left to come to you; but see, it is now dry and crumbly.

¹³ These wineskins were new when we filled them; but see, they are cracked. And these clothes and sandals of ours are worn out from the extremely long journey." ¹⁴ Then the men of Israel took some of their provisions, but did not seek the LORD's decision. ¹⁵ So Joshua established peace with them and made a treaty to let them live, and the leaders of the community swore an oath to them.

GIBEON'S DECEPTION DISCOVERED

¹⁶ Three days after making the treaty with them, they heard that the Gibeonites were their neighbors, living among them. ¹⁷ So the Israelites set out and reached the Gibeonite cities on the third day. Now their cities were Gibeon, Chephirah, Beeroth, and Kiriath-jearim. ¹⁸ But the Israelites did not attack them, because the leaders of the community had sworn an oath to them by the LORD, the God of Israel. Then the whole community grumbled against the leaders.

¹⁹ All the leaders answered them, "We have sworn an oath to them by the LORD, the God of Israel, and now we cannot touch them. ²⁰ This is how we will

treat them: we will let them live, so that no wrath will fall on us because of the oath we swore to them." ²¹ They also said, "Let them live." So the Gibeonites became woodcutters and water carriers for the whole community, as the leaders had promised them.

²² Joshua summoned the Gibeonites and said to them, "Why did you deceive us by telling us you live far away from us, when in fact you live among us? ²³ Therefore you are cursed and will always be slaves—woodcutters and water carriers for the house of my God."

²⁴ The Gibeonites answered him, "It was clearly communicated to your servants that the LORD your God had commanded his servant Moses to give you all the land and to destroy all the inhabitants of the land before you. We greatly feared for our lives because of you, and that is why we did this. ²⁵ Now we are in your hands. Do to us whatever you think is right." ²⁶ This is what Joshua did to them: he rescued them from the Israelites, and they did not kill them. ²⁷ On that day he made them woodcutters and water carriers—as they are today—for the community and for the LORD's altar at the place he would choose.

THE DAY THE SUN STOOD STILL

10 Now King Adoni-zedek of Jerusalem heard that Joshua had captured Ai and completely destroyed it, treating Ai and its king as he had Jericho and its king, and that the inhabitants of Gibeon had made peace with Israel and were living among them. ² So Adoni-zedek and his people were greatly alarmed because Gibeon was a large city like one of the royal cities; it was larger than Ai, and all its men were warriors. ³ Therefore King Adoni-zedek of Jerusalem sent word to King Hoham of Hebron, King Piram of Jarmuth, King Japhia of Lachish, and King Debir of Eglon, saying, ⁴ "Come up and help me. We will attack Gibeon, because they have made peace with Joshua and the Israelites." ⁵ So the five Amorite kings—the kings of Jerusalem, Hebron, Jarmuth, Lachish, and Eglon—joined forces, advanced with all their armies, besieged Gibeon, and fought against it.

⁶ Then the men of Gibeon sent word to Joshua in the camp at Gilgal: "Don't give up on your servants. Come quickly and save us! Help us, for all the Amorite kings living in the hill country have joined forces against us." ⁷ So Joshua and all his troops, including all his best soldiers, came from Gilgal. ⁸ The LORD said to Joshua, "Do not be afraid of them, for I have handed them over to you. Not one of them will be able to stand against you."

⁹ So Joshua caught them by surprise, after marching all night from Gilgal. ¹⁰ The LORD threw them into confusion before Israel. He defeated them in a great slaughter at Gibeon, chased them through the ascent of Beth-horon, and struck them down as far as Azekah and Makkedah. ¹¹ As they fled before Israel, the LORD threw large hailstones on them from the sky along the descent of Beth-horon all the way to Azekah, and they died. More of them died from the hail than the Israelites killed with the sword.

¹² On the day the LORD gave the Amorites over to the Israelites, Joshua spoke to the LORD in the presence of Israel:

"Sun, stand still over Gibeon,
and moon, over the Valley of Aijalon."
¹³ And the sun stood still
and the moon stopped
until the nation took vengeance on its enemies.
Isn't this written in the Book of Jashar?
So the sun stopped
in the middle of the sky
and delayed its setting
almost a full day.
¹⁴ There has been no day like it before or since, when the LORD listened to a man, because the LORD fought for Israel. ¹⁵ Then Joshua and all Israel with him returned to the camp at Gilgal.

EXECUTION OF THE FIVE KINGS

¹⁶ Now the five defeated kings had fled and hidden in the cave at Makkedah. ¹⁷ It was reported to Joshua, "The five kings have been found; they are hiding in the cave at Makkedah." ¹⁸ Joshua said, "Roll large stones against the mouth of the cave, and station men by it to guard the kings. ¹⁹ But as for the rest of you, don't stay there. Pursue your enemies and attack them from behind. Don't let them enter their cities, for the LORD your God has handed them over to you." ²⁰ So Joshua and the Israelites finished inflicting a terrible slaughter on them until they were destroyed, although a few survivors ran away to the fortified cities. ²¹ The people returned safely to Joshua in the camp at Makkedah. And no one dared to threaten the Israelites.

²² Then Joshua said, "Open the mouth of the cave, and bring those five kings to me out of there." ²³ That is what they did. They brought the five kings of Jerusalem, Hebron, Jarmuth, Lachish, and Eglon to Joshua out of the cave. ²⁴ When they had brought the kings to him, Joshua summoned all the men of Israel and said to the military commanders who had accompanied him, "Come here and put your feet on the necks of these kings." So the commanders came forward and put their feet on their necks. ²⁵ Joshua said to them, "Do not be afraid or discouraged. Be strong and courageous, for the LORD will do this to all the enemies you fight."

²⁶ After this, Joshua struck them down and executed them. He hung their bodies on five trees and they were there until evening. ²⁷ At sunset Joshua commanded that they be taken down from the trees and thrown into the cave where they had hidden. Then large stones were placed against the mouth of the cave, and the stones are still there today.

CONQUEST OF THE SOUTHERN CITIES

²⁸ On that day Joshua captured Makkedah and struck it down with the sword, including its king. He completely destroyed it and everyone in it, leaving no survivors. So he treated the king of Makkedah as he had the king of Jericho.

Week 5: Leaving Nothing Undone

⁲⁹ Joshua and all Israel with him crossed from Makkedah to Libnah and fought against Libnah. ³⁰ The LORD also handed it and its king over to Israel. He struck it down, putting everyone in it to the sword, and left no survivors in it. He treated Libnah's king as he had the king of Jericho.

³¹ From Libnah, Joshua and all Israel with him crossed to Lachish. They laid siege to it and attacked it. ³² The LORD handed Lachish over to Israel, and Joshua captured it on the second day. He struck it down, putting everyone in it to the sword, just as he had done to Libnah. ³³ At that time King Horam of Gezer went to help Lachish, but Joshua struck him down along with his people, leaving no survivors.

³⁴ Then Joshua crossed from Lachish to Eglon and all Israel with him. They laid siege to it and attacked it. ³⁵ On that day they captured it and struck it down, putting everyone in it to the sword. He completely destroyed it that day, just as he had done to Lachish.

³⁶ Next, Joshua and all Israel with him went up from Eglon to Hebron and attacked it. ³⁷ They captured it and struck down its king, all its villages, and everyone in it with the sword. He left no survivors, just as he had done at Eglon. He completely destroyed Hebron and everyone in it.

³⁸ Finally, Joshua turned toward Debir and attacked it. And all Israel was with him. ³⁹ He captured it—its king and all its villages. They struck them down with the sword and completely destroyed everyone in it, leaving no survivors. He treated Debir and its king as he had treated Hebron and as he had treated Libnah and its king.

⁴⁰ So Joshua conquered the whole region—the hill country, the Negev, the Judean foothills, and the slopes—with all their kings, leaving no survivors. He completely destroyed every living being, as the LORD, the God of Israel, had commanded. ⁴¹ Joshua conquered everyone from Kadesh-barnea to Gaza, and all the land of Goshen as far as Gibeon. ⁴² Joshua captured all these kings and their land in one campaign, because the LORD, the God of Israel, fought for Israel. ⁴³ Then Joshua returned with all Israel to the camp at Gilgal.

CONQUEST OF THE NORTHERN CITIES

11 When King Jabin of Hazor heard this news, he sent a message to: King Jobab of Madon, the kings of Shimron and Achshaph, ² and the kings of the north in the hill country, the Arabah south of Chinnereth, the Judean foothills, and the Slopes of Dor to the west, ³ the Canaanites in the east and west, the Amorites, Hethites, Perizzites, and Jebusites in the hill country, and the Hivites at the foot of Hermon in the land of Mizpah. ⁴ They went out with all their armies—a multitude as numerous as the sand on the seashore—along with a vast number of horses and chariots. ⁵ All these kings joined forces; they came and camped together at the Waters of Merom to attack Israel.

⁶ The LORD said to Joshua, "Do not be afraid of them, for at this time tomorrow I will cause all of them to be killed before Israel. You are to hamstring their horses and burn their chariots."

⁷ So Joshua and all his troops surprised them at the Waters of Merom and attacked them.
⁸ The LORD handed them over to Israel, and they struck them down, pursuing them as far as greater Sidon and Misrephoth-maim, and to the east as far as the Valley of Mizpeh. They struck them down, leaving no survivors. ⁹ Joshua treated them as the LORD had told him; he hamstrung their horses and burned their chariots.
¹⁰ At that time Joshua turned back, captured Hazor, and struck down its king with the sword, because Hazor had formerly been the leader of all these kingdoms. ¹¹ They struck down everyone in it with the sword, completely destroying them; he left no one alive. Then he burned Hazor.
¹² Joshua captured all these kings and their cities and struck them down with the sword. He completely destroyed them, as Moses the LORD's servant had commanded. ¹³ However, Israel did not burn any of the cities that stood on their mounds except Hazor, which Joshua burned. ¹⁴ The Israelites plundered all the spoils and cattle of these cities for themselves. But they struck down every person with the sword until they had annihilated them, leaving no one alive. ¹⁵ Just as the LORD had commanded his servant Moses, Moses commanded Joshua. That is what Joshua did, leaving nothing undone of all that the LORD had commanded Moses.

SUMMARY OF THE CONQUESTS

¹⁶ So Joshua took all this land—the hill country, all the Negev, all the land of Goshen, the foothills, the Arabah, and the hill country of Israel with its foothills— ¹⁷ from Mount Halak, which ascends to Seir, as far as Baal-gad in the Valley of Lebanon at the foot of Mount Hermon. He captured all their kings and struck them down, putting them to death. ¹⁸ Joshua waged war with all these kings for a long time. ¹⁹ No city made peace with the Israelites except the Hivites who inhabited Gibeon; all of them were taken in battle. ²⁰ For it was the LORD's intention to harden their hearts, so that they would engage Israel in battle, be completely destroyed without mercy, and be annihilated, just as the LORD had commanded Moses.
²¹ At that time Joshua proceeded to exterminate the Anakim from the hill country—Hebron, Debir, Anab—all the hill country of Judah and of Israel. Joshua completely destroyed them with their cities. ²² No Anakim were left in the land of the Israelites, except for some remaining in Gaza, Gath, and Ashdod.
²³ So Joshua took the entire land, in keeping with all that the LORD had told Moses. Joshua then gave it as an inheritance to Israel according to their tribal allotments. After this, the land had rest from war.

TERRITORY EAST OF THE JORDAN

12 The Israelites struck down the following kings of the land and took possession of their land beyond the Jordan to the east and from the Arnon River to Mount Hermon, including all the Arabah eastward:

Week 5: Leaving Nothing Undone

2 King Sihon of the Amorites lived in Heshbon. He ruled from Aroer on the rim of the Arnon River, along the middle of the valley, and half of Gilead up to the Jabbok River (the border of the Ammonites), 3 the Arabah east of the Sea of Chinnereth to the Sea of Arabah (that is, the Dead Sea), eastward through Beth-jeshimoth and southward below the slopes of Pisgah.
4 King Og of Bashan, of the remnant of the Rephaim, lived in Ashtaroth and Edrei. 5 He ruled over Mount Hermon, Salecah, all Bashan up to the Geshurite and Maacathite border, and half of Gilead to the border of King Sihon of Heshbon. 6 Moses the LORD's servant and the Israelites struck them down. And Moses the LORD's servant gave their land as an inheritance to the Reubenites, Gadites, and half the tribe of Manasseh.

TERRITORY WEST OF THE JORDAN
7 Joshua and the Israelites struck down the following kings of the land beyond the Jordan to the west, from Baal-gad in the Valley of Lebanon to Mount Halak, which ascends toward Seir (Joshua gave their land as an inheritance to the tribes of Israel according to their allotments:
8 the hill country, the Judean foothills, the Arabah, the slopes, the wilderness, and the Negev—the lands of the Hethites, Amorites, Canaanites, Perizzites, Hivites, and Jebusites):

9 the king of Jericho	one
the king of Ai, which is next to Bethel	one
10 the king of Jerusalem	one
the king of Hebron	one
11 the king of Jarmuth	one
the king of Lachish	one
12 the king of Eglon	one
the king of Gezer	one
13 the king of Debir	one
the king of Geder	one
14 the king of Hormah	one
the king of Arad	one
15 the king of Libnah	one
the king of Adullam	one
16 the king of Makkedah	one
the king of Bethel	one
17 the king of Tappuah	one
the king of Hepher	one
18 the king of Aphek	one
the king of Lasharon	one
19 the king of Madon	one
the king of Hazor	one
20 the king of Shimron-meron	one
the king of Achshaph	one

²¹ the king of Taanach	one
the king of Megiddo	one
²² the king of Kedesh	one
the king of Jokneam in Carmel	one
²³ the king of Dor in Naphath-dor	one
the king of Goiim in Gilgal	one
²⁴ the king of Tirzah	one
the total number of all kings:	thirty-one.

Week 5: Leaving Nothing Undone

Comprehend

In this section, we will examine closely what the Biblical text <u>says</u>. These questions are designed to help you notice and retain important details from this section of Scripture.

1. What action did the kings west of the Jordan take after hearing about the events at Jericho and Ai? (9:2)

2. The Gibeonites took a different approach. Summarize their plan. (9:3-6)

3. What did the Israelites fail to do in Joshua 9:14?

4. What reason did the Gibeonites provide when Joshua questioned them regarding their deception? (9:24)

5. As Chapter 10 opens, what did the five Amorite kings do and why? (10:4)[3]

6. What assurance did God give Joshua? (10:8)

7. Look closely at Joshua 10:9-14. Use the space below to make notes regarding the following:

Actions taken by Joshua / the Israelites	Actions taken by the Lord

8. When the five kings were found, Joshua did not deal with them right away. Instead, what did he have the Israelites do? (10:19)

9. How did Joshua use the defeat of the five kings to encourage the Israelite commanders? (10:25)

---
[3] See the *Southern and Northern Campaigns* map on p. 164

Joshua   PURSUING THE PROMISES OF GOD

10. What consistent message is given regarding the outcome of the battles described in Joshua 10:28-43?[4]

11. According to Joshua 10:42, why was Joshua able to capture all these kings and their land in one campaign?

12. How did the kings of the north react to the news of the Israelites' defeat of the southern cities? (11:4-5)[4]

13. What was the outcome of these battles? (11:12)

14. Fill in the blanks from Joshua 11:15:

    That is what Joshua did, leaving _____ undone of _____ that the LORD had commanded Moses.

15. Joshua 11:20 tells us that it was the Lord's intention to harden the hearts of the inhabitants of the land.

    a. What did the inhabitants of the land do as a result of their hardened hearts?

    b. What was the ultimate outcome?

16. What did Joshua do with the land? (11:23)

17. Chapter 12 recaps the battles Israel had won to date.

    a. Who had led the Israelites in conquering the territory east of the Jordan? (12:6)

    b. Who had led the Israelites in conquering the territory west of the Jordan? (12:7)

18. Summarize the primary focus of this section of Scripture in a single sentence.

---
[4] See the *Southern and Northern Campaigns* map on p. 164

Week 5: Leaving Nothing Undone

Interpret

In this section, we will be studying to discover what the text means. These questions focus your attention on specific details, draw from other parts of the Bible to improve understanding, and highlight the bigger story of Scripture.

1. Review your highlights and underlines from the Read with Purpose section.

    a. Briefly summarize the Lord's activity:

    b. What characteristics of God did you notice? You can reference the list of attributes provided on pp. 160-161 for help.

2. When the Gibeonites heard about the defeat of Jericho and Ai, they acted deceptively in order to secure peace with Israel and avoid the same fate.

    a. What could the Israelites have done to avoid being bound to this oath? (Consider Joshua 2:17-20 and 9:14.)

    b. What can we learn about God from the fact that He did not intervene in the situation or prevent the treaty?

3. Despite the Gibeonites' deception, the Israelite leaders would not break their oath; they believed God's wrath would fall on them if they did so.

    a. Read 2 Samuel 21:1-2 and note why this fear was warranted.

    b. The Israelites' failure to "seek the Lord's decision" put them in a situation where there was no way to fully obey God. What takeaways do you have from this situation?

4. Whereas the Gibeonites sought peace, the Amorite kings attacked. In a key battle, Joshua boldly asked God to cause the sun to stand still and God did so!

    a. Consider the timing. Why might God have chosen to do this miracle at this time?

    b. How do the following passages help you better understand why God performs miracles?

    Job 37:5-7

    Matthew 21:21-22

    1 John 5:14-15

5. Joshua 11:19 tells us that of all the inhabitants of Canaan, only the Gibeonites sought peace and were spared God's judgment.

    a. Read Romans 5:1. How can humanity obtain peace with God?

    b. In order to obtain peace, the Gibeonites surrendered their cities and became Israel's servants. Read Romans 6:16-23. How does this point to what humanity must do?

6. The rest of Canaan persisted in rebellion and although God was patient with them, His patience did not last forever. Read the passages below and summarize their warnings to humanity.

    Isaiah 55:6-7

    Proverbs 1:23-31

    Romans 2:4-6

Week 5: Leaving Nothing Undone

7. In Chapter 11, God had the Israelites maim horses and destroy chariots that could have been useful to them in their continued battles.

    a. Read Isaiah 31:1. What insight does this passage provide as to why God might have had the Israelites do this?

    b. What can believers learn from this?

8. Joshua set an example for all believers as he left "nothing undone" of all God commanded. Fill in the *Godly Leadership* exhibit on p. 163 with information from this week's study.

9. In this week's passage, the Israelites followed God's lead as they engaged in many battles for their inheritance.

    a. What practical lessons can believers learn about following God's lead from Joshua and the Israelites?

    b. The Israelites battled in pursuit of God's promises, as must believers. Fill in the table below regarding our battles.

Passage	What we fight against	How we are to fight
Galatians 5:24-25		
2 Corinthians 10:3-5		
Titus 2:11-12		
Ephesians 6:10-18		

77

Joshua PURSUING THE PROMISES OF GOD

Apply

In this section, we'll consider ways in which God is speaking to us personally. The questions to the left focus on major themes and topics from this week of study. You can use those, or anything else the Lord brought to your attention, to answer the following:

God wants His people to seek Him. How can you more consistently seek the Lord's decision?

God responds to our requests. Has He brought to mind any areas where you should be more bold in your prayers?

The Israelites battled for a long time. How does this encourage you in the spiritual battles you face?

The enemy's attacks preceded huge victories for the Israelites. How does that shift your perspective? How can you better capitalize on times when you are being attacked?

Recognize His voice:
What did the Lord draw your attention to this week?

Respond to what He has said:
How can you respond?

Week 5: Leaving Nothing Undone

Final Thoughts
Use the space below to record any questions or takeaways you have regarding this week's material.

Repetitive Reading
It is of great benefit to repetitively read Scripture. Quickly read (or skim through) the entire book of Joshua at the end of each week of study. Record anything that stands out to you.

Pray
Think about what you have learned this week. Close by responding to the Lord in prayer.

LEAN IN

Notes from small group discussion:

Week 5: Leaving Nothing Undone

LEARN

Notes from teaching session:

An Unconquered Inheritance

WEEK 6

Week 6: An Unconquered Inheritance

LISTEN

Pray
God is faithful; He gives His people an inheritance and keeps them as His own. Begin your time of study in prayer. Thank God for the gift of His inheritance. Humbly ask Him to give you the strength and courage necessary to take hold of it.

> *I pray that the eyes of your heart may be enlightened so that you may know what is the hope of his calling, what is the wealth of his glorious inheritance in the saints, and what is the immeasurable greatness of his power toward us who believe, according to the mighty working of his strength.*
> Ephesians 1:18-19

Reflect
From the past week of study, what had the most significant impact on you?

Read with Purpose
The Bible is primarily a book about God. As you read the passage of Scripture for Week 6 (Joshua Chapters 13-17), look first for what God says and does. Using the copy of the text on the pages that follow, *highlight in blue* everything God says, and *underline in blue* everything God does.

Note: This week's passage is fairly long. Your aim for Read with Purpose should be to read the text quickly, preferably in one sitting.

Joshua 13-17

UNCONQUERED LANDS

13 Joshua was now old, advanced in age, and the LORD said to him, "You have become old, advanced in age, but a great deal of the land remains to be possessed. ² This is the land that remains: All the districts of the Philistines and the Geshurites: ³ from the Shihor east of Egypt to the border of Ekron on the north (considered to be Canaanite territory)—the five Philistine rulers of Gaza, Ashdod, Ashkelon, Gath, and Ekron, as well as the Avvites ⁴ in the south; all the land of the Canaanites, from Arah of the Sidonians to Aphek and as far as the border of the Amorites; ⁵ the land of the Gebalites; and all Lebanon east from Baal-gad below Mount Hermon to the entrance of Hamath— ⁶ all the inhabitants of the hill country from Lebanon to Misrephoth-maim, all the Sidonians. I will drive them out before the Israelites, only distribute the land as an inheritance for Israel, as I have commanded you. ⁷ Therefore, divide this land as an inheritance to the nine tribes and half the tribe of Manasseh."

THE INHERITANCE EAST OF THE JORDAN

⁸ With the other half of the tribe of Manasseh, the Reubenites and Gadites had received the inheritance Moses gave them beyond the Jordan to the east, just as Moses the LORD's servant had given them:

⁹ From Aroer on the rim of the Arnon Valley, along with the city in the middle of the valley, all the Medeba plateau as far as Dibon, ¹⁰ and all the cities of King Sihon of the Amorites, who reigned in Heshbon, to the border of the Ammonites; ¹¹ also Gilead and the territory of the Geshurites and Maacathites, all Mount Hermon, and all Bashan to Salecah— ¹² the whole kingdom of Og in Bashan, who reigned in Ashtaroth and Edrei; he was one of the remaining Rephaim.

Moses struck them down and drove them out, ¹³ but the Israelites did not drive out the Geshurites and Maacathites. So Geshur and Maacath still live in Israel today.

¹⁴ He did not, however, give any inheritance to the tribe of Levi. This was their inheritance, just as he had promised: the food offerings made to the LORD, the God of Israel.

REUBEN'S INHERITANCE

¹⁵ To the tribe of Reuben's descendants by their clans, Moses gave ¹⁶ this as their territory:

From Aroer on the rim of the Arnon Valley, along with the city in the middle of the valley, the whole plateau as far as Medeba, ¹⁷ with Heshbon and all its cities on the plateau—Dibon, Bamoth-baal, Beth-baal-meon, ¹⁸ Jahaz, Kedemoth, Mephaath, ¹⁹ Kiriathaim, Sibmah, Zereth-shahar on the hill in the valley, ²⁰ Beth-peor, the slopes of Pisgah, and Beth-jeshimoth— ²¹ all the cities of the plateau, and all the kingdom of King Sihon of the Amorites, who reigned in Heshbon. Moses had killed him and the chiefs of Midian—Evi, Rekem, Zur, Hur, and Reba—the princes of Sihon who lived in the land. ²² Along with those the Israelites put to death, they also killed the diviner, Balaam son of Beor, with the sword.

²³ The border of the Reubenites was the Jordan and its plain. This was the inheritance of the Reubenites by their clans, with the cities and their settlements.

GAD'S INHERITANCE

²⁴ To the tribe of the Gadites by their clans, Moses gave ²⁵ this as their territory: Jazer and all the cities of Gilead, and half the land of the Ammonites to Aroer, near Rabbah;

²⁶ from Heshbon to Ramath-mizpeh and Betonim, and from Mahanaim to the border of Debir; ²⁷ in the valley: Beth-haram, Beth-nimrah, Succoth, and Zaphon—the rest of the kingdom of King Sihon of Heshbon. Their land also included the Jordan and its territory as far as the edge of the Sea of Chinnereth on the east side of the Jordan.

²⁸ This was the inheritance of the Gadites by their clans, with the cities and their settlements.

EAST MANASSEH'S INHERITANCE

²⁹ And to half the tribe of Manasseh (that is, to half the tribe of Manasseh's descendants by their clans) Moses gave ³⁰ this as their territory:

From Mahanaim through all Bashan—all the kingdom of King Og of Bashan, including all of Jair's Villages that are in Bashan—sixty cities. ³¹ But half of Gilead, and Og's royal cities in Bashan—Ashtaroth and Edrei—are for the descendants of Machir son of Manasseh (that is, half the descendants of Machir by their clans).

³² These were the portions Moses gave them on the plains of Moab beyond the Jordan east of Jericho. ³³ But Moses did not give a portion to the tribe of Levi. The LORD, the God of Israel, was their inheritance, just as he had promised them.

ISRAEL'S INHERITANCE IN CANAAN

14 The Israelites received these portions that the priest Eleazar, Joshua son of Nun, and the family heads of the Israelite tribes gave them in the land of Canaan. ² Their inheritance was by lot as the LORD commanded through Moses for the nine and a half tribes, ³ because Moses had given the inheritance to the two and a half tribes beyond the Jordan. But he gave no inheritance among them to the Levites. ⁴ The descendants of Joseph became two tribes, Manasseh and Ephraim. No portion of the land was given to the Levites except cities to live in, along with pasturelands for their cattle and livestock. ⁵ So the Israelites did as the LORD commanded Moses, and they divided the land.

CALEB'S INHERITANCE

⁶ The descendants of Judah approached Joshua at Gilgal, and Caleb son of Jephunneh the Kenizzite said to him, "You know what the LORD promised Moses the man of God at Kadesh-barnea about you and me. ⁷ I was forty years old when Moses the LORD's servant sent me from Kadesh-barnea to scout the land, and I brought back an honest report. ⁸ My brothers who went with me caused the people to lose heart, but I followed the LORD my God completely. ⁹ On that day Moses swore to me, 'The land where you have set foot will be an inheritance for you and your descendants forever, because you have followed the LORD my God completely.'

¹⁰ "As you see, the LORD has kept me alive these forty-five years as he promised, since the LORD spoke this word to Moses while Israel was journeying in the wilderness. Here I am today, eighty-five years old. ¹¹ I am still as strong today as I was the day Moses sent me out. My strength for battle and for daily tasks is now as it was then. ¹² Now give me this hill country the LORD promised me on that day, because you heard then that the Anakim are there, as well as large fortified cities. Perhaps the LORD will be with me and I will drive them out as the LORD promised."

¹³ Then Joshua blessed Caleb son of Jephunneh and gave him Hebron as an inheritance.

¹⁴ Therefore, Hebron still belongs to Caleb son of Jephunneh the Kenizzite as an inheritance today because he followed the LORD, the God of Israel, completely. ¹⁵ Hebron's name used to be Kiriath-arba; Arba was the greatest man among the Anakim. After this, the land had rest from war.

JUDAH'S INHERITANCE

15 Now the allotment for the tribe of the descendants of Judah by their clans was in the southernmost region, south to the Wilderness of Zin and over to the border of Edom.

² Their southern border began at the tip of the Dead Sea on the south bay ³ and went south of the Scorpions' Ascent, proceeded to Zin, ascended to the south of Kadesh-barnea, passed Hezron, ascended to Addar, and turned to Karka. ⁴ It proceeded to Azmon and to the Brook of Egypt and so the border ended at the Mediterranean Sea. This is your southern border.

⁵ Now the eastern border was along the Dead Sea to the mouth of the Jordan.

The border on the north side was from the bay of the sea at the mouth of the Jordan. ⁶ It ascended to Beth-hoglah, proceeded north of Beth-arabah, and ascended to the Stone of Bohan son of Reuben. ⁷ Then the border ascended to Debir from the Valley of Achor, turning north to the Gilgal that is opposite the Ascent of Adummim, which is south of the ravine. The border proceeded to the Waters of En-shemesh and ended at En-rogel.

⁸ From there the border ascended Ben Hinnom Valley to the southern Jebusite slope (that is, Jerusalem) and ascended to the top of the hill that faces Hinnom Valley on the west, at the northern end of Rephaim Valley.

⁹ From the top of the hill the border curved to the spring of the Waters of Nephtoah, went to the cities of Mount Ephron, and then curved to Baalah (that is, Kiriath-jearim). ¹⁰ The border turned westward from Baalah to Mount Seir, went to the northern slope of Mount Jearim (that is, Chesalon), descended to Beth-shemesh, and proceeded to Timnah. ¹¹ Then the border reached to the slope north of Ekron, curved to Shikkeron, proceeded to Mount Baalah, went to Jabneel, and ended at the Mediterranean Sea.
¹² Now the western border was the coastline of the Mediterranean Sea. This was the boundary of the descendants of Judah around their clans.

CALEB AND OTHNIEL

¹³ He gave Caleb son of Jephunneh the following portion among the descendants of Judah based on the LORD's instruction to Joshua: Kiriath-arba (that is, Hebron; Arba was the father of Anak). ¹⁴ Caleb drove out from there the three sons of Anak: Sheshai, Ahiman, and Talmai, descendants of Anak. ¹⁵ From there he marched against the inhabitants of Debir, which used to be called Kiriath-sepher, ¹⁶ and Caleb said, "Whoever attacks and captures Kiriath-sepher, I will give my daughter Achsah to him as a wife." ¹⁷ So Othniel son of Caleb's brother, Kenaz, captured it, and Caleb gave his daughter Achsah to him as a wife. ¹⁸ When she arrived, she persuaded Othniel to ask her father for a field. As she got off her donkey, Caleb asked her, "What can I do for you?" ¹⁹ She replied, "Give me a blessing. Since you have given me land in the Negev, give me the springs also." So he gave her the upper and lower springs.

JUDAH'S CITITES

²⁰ This was the inheritance of the tribe of the descendants of Judah by their clans.

²¹ These were the outermost cities of the tribe of the descendants of Judah toward the border of Edom in the Negev: Kabzeel, Eder, Jagur, ²² Kinah, Dimonah, Adadah, ²³ Kedesh, Hazor, Ithnan, ²⁴ Ziph, Telem, Bealoth, ²⁵ Hazor-hadattah, Kerioth-hezron (that is, Hazor), ²⁶ Amam, Shema, Moladah, ²⁷ Hazar-gaddah, Heshmon, Beth-pelet, ²⁸ Hazar-shual, Beer-sheba, Biziothiah, ²⁹ Baalah, Iim, Ezem, ³⁰ Eltolad, Chesil, Hormah, ³¹ Ziklag, Madmannah, Sansannah, ³² Lebaoth, Shilhim, Ain, and Rimmon—twenty-nine cities in all, with their settlements.
³³ In the Judean foothills: Eshtaol, Zorah, Ashnah, ³⁴ Zanoah, En-gannim, Tappuah, Enam, ³⁵ Jarmuth, Adullam, Socoh, Azekah, ³⁶ Shaaraim, Adithaim, Gederah, and Gederothaim—fourteen cities, with their settlements; ³⁷ Zenan, Hadashah, Migdal-gad, ³⁸ Dilan, Mizpeh, Jokthe-el, ³⁹ Lachish, Bozkath, Eglon, ⁴⁰ Cabbon, Lahmam, Chitlish, ⁴¹ Gederoth, Beth-dagon, Naamah, and Makkedah—sixteen cities, with their settlements; ⁴² Libnah, Ether, Ashan, ⁴³ Iphtah, Ashnah, Nezib, ⁴⁴ Keilah, Achzib, and Mareshah—nine cities, with their settlements; ⁴⁵ Ekron, with its surrounding villages and settlements; ⁴⁶ from Ekron to the sea, all the cities near Ashdod, with their settlements; ⁴⁷ Ashdod, with its surrounding villages and settlements; Gaza, with its

surrounding villages and settlements, to the Brook of Egypt and the coastline of the Mediterranean Sea.

⁴⁸ In the hill country: Shamir, Jattir, Socoh, ⁴⁹ Dannah, Kiriath-sannah (that is, Debir), ⁵⁰ Anab, Eshtemoh, Anim, ⁵¹ Goshen, Holon, and Giloh—eleven cities, with their settlements; ⁵² Arab, Dumah, Eshan, ⁵³ Janim, Beth-tappuah, Aphekah, ⁵⁴ Humtah, Kiriath-arba (that is, Hebron), and Zior—nine cities, with their settlements; ⁵⁵ Maon, Carmel, Ziph, Juttah, ⁵⁶ Jezreel, Jokdeam, Zanoah, ⁵⁷ Kain, Gibeah, and Timnah—ten cities, with their settlements; ⁵⁸ Halhul, Beth-zur, Gedor, ⁵⁹ Maarath, Beth-anoth, and Eltekon—six cities, with their settlements; ⁶⁰ Kiriath-baal (that is, Kiriath-jearim), and Rabbah—two cities, with their settlements.

⁶¹ In the wilderness: Beth-arabah, Middin, Secacah, ⁶² Nibshan, the City of Salt, and En-gedi—six cities, with their settlements.

⁶³ But the descendants of Judah could not drive out the Jebusites who lived in Jerusalem. So the Jebusites still live in Jerusalem among the descendants of Judah today.

JOSEPH'S INHERITANCE

16 The allotment for the descendants of Joseph went from the Jordan at Jericho to the Waters of Jericho on the east, through the wilderness ascending from Jericho into the hill country of Bethel. ² From Bethel it went to Luz and proceeded to the border of the Archites by Ataroth. ³ It then descended westward to the border of the Japhletites as far as the border of Lower Beth-horon, then to Gezer, and ended at the Mediterranean Sea. ⁴ So Ephraim and Manasseh, the sons of Joseph, received their inheritance.

EPHRAIM'S INHERITANCE

⁵ This was the territory of the descendants of Ephraim by their clans:
The border of their inheritance went from Ataroth-addar on the east to Upper Beth-horon. ⁶ In the north the border went westward from Michmethath; it turned eastward from Taanath-shiloh and passed it east of Janoah. ⁷ From Janoah it descended to Ataroth and Naarah, and then reached Jericho and went to the Jordan. ⁸ From Tappuah the border went westward along the Brook of Kanah and ended at the Mediterranean Sea.
This was the inheritance of the tribe of the descendants of Ephraim by their clans, together with ⁹ the cities set apart for the descendants of Ephraim within the inheritance of the descendants of Manasseh—all these cities with their settlements. ¹⁰ However, they did not drive out the Canaanites who lived in Gezer. So the Canaanites still live in Ephraim today, but they are forced laborers.

WEST MANASSEH'S INHERITANCE

17 This was the allotment for the tribe of Manasseh as Joseph's firstborn. Gilead and Bashan were given to Machir, the firstborn of Manasseh and the father of Gilead, because he was a man of war. ² So the allotment was for the rest of Manasseh's descendants by their clans, for the sons of Abiezer, Helek, Asriel, Shechem, Hepher, and Shemida. These are the male descendants of Manasseh son of Joseph, by their clans. ³ Now Zelophehad son of Hepher, son of Gilead, son of Machir, son of Manasseh, had no sons, only daughters. These are the names of his daughters: Mahlah, Noah, Hoglah, Milcah, and Tirzah. ⁴ They came before the priest Eleazar, Joshua son of Nun, and the leaders, saying, "The LORD commanded Moses to give us an inheritance among our male relatives." So they gave them an inheritance among their father's brothers, in keeping with the LORD's instruction. ⁵ As a result, ten tracts fell to Manasseh, besides the land of Gilead and Bashan, which are beyond the Jordan, ⁶ because Manasseh's daughters received an inheritance among his sons. The land of Gilead belonged to the rest of Manasseh's sons.

⁷ The border of Manasseh went from Asher to Michmethath near Shechem. It then went southward toward the inhabitants of En-tappuah. ⁸ The region of Tappuah belonged to Manasseh, but Tappuah itself on Manasseh's border belonged to the descendants of Ephraim. ⁹ From there the border descended to the Brook of Kanah; south of the brook, cities belonged to Ephraim among Manasseh's cities. Manasseh's border was on the north side of the brook and ended at the Mediterranean Sea. ¹⁰ Ephraim's territory was to the south and Manasseh's to the north, with the Sea as its border. They reached Asher on the north and Issachar on the east. ¹¹ Within Issachar and Asher, Manasseh had Beth-shean, Ibleam, and the inhabitants of Dor with their surrounding villages; the inhabitants of En-dor, Taanach, and Megiddo—the three cities of Naphath—with their surrounding villages.

¹² The descendants of Manasseh could not possess these cities, because the Canaanites were determined to stay in this land. ¹³ However, when the Israelites grew stronger, they imposed forced labor on the Canaanites but did not drive them out completely.

JOSEPH'S ADDITIONAL INHERITANCE

¹⁴ Joseph's descendants said to Joshua, "Why did you give us only one tribal allotment as an inheritance? We have many people, because the LORD has been blessing us greatly."

¹⁵ "If you have so many people," Joshua replied to them, "go to the forest and clear an area for yourselves there in the land of the Perizzites and the Rephaim, because Ephraim's hill country is too small for you."

¹⁶ But the descendants of Joseph said, "The hill country is not enough for us, and all the Canaanites who inhabit the valley area have iron chariots, both at Beth-shean with its surrounding villages and in the Jezreel Valley."

¹⁷ So Joshua replied to Joseph's family (that is, Ephraim and Manasseh), "You

have many people and great strength. You will not have just one allotment, [18] because the hill country will be yours also. It is a forest; clear it and its outlying areas will be yours. You can also drive out the Canaanites, even though they have iron chariots and are strong."

Week 6: An Unconquered Inheritance

Comprehend

In this section, we will examine closely what the Biblical text <u>says</u>. These questions are designed to help you notice and retain important details from this section of Scripture.

1. What observation did the Lord make about the land in Joshua 13:1?

2. From Joshua 13:6:

    a. What did God say He would do regarding the inhabitants of the land?

    b. What was the "only" thing God commanded Joshua to do?

3. In Joshua 13:7, the Lord commanded Joshua to "divide this land as an inheritance to the nine tribes and half the tribe of Manasseh."

    a. Which tribes had *already* received their inheritance? (13:8)

    b. Who had distributed this land to them? (13:8)

    c. Where was the land that had been distributed to these two and a half tribes? (13:8)

4. Did the Israelites completely drive out the people of the land east of the Jordan? (13:13)

    Yes   No

5. Throughout this week's text, we were repeatedly told that the Levites would not receive land as an inheritance. Use Joshua 13:14, 13:33 and 14:4 to fill in the block next to "Levi" on the *Family of Israel* visual on p. 159 with what *would* be their inheritance

6. Joshua Chapter 14 began with the distribution of the land *west* of the Jordan, in Canaan.

    a. Who was responsible for the distribution of this land? (14:1)

    b. How was the division of the inheritance of these tribes determined? (14:2)

7. Of what are we reminded regarding the descendants of Joseph in Joshua 14:4?[5]

8. As the descendants of Judah approached Joshua, Caleb spoke first. Note below how he characterized what happened when Israel first approached the Promised Land 45 years earlier.

   a. What had Caleb done? (14:7-8)

   b. What had the other spies done? (14:8)

9. What did Caleb say the Lord had done for him? (14:10-11)

10. What did Caleb ask for and why? (14:12)

11. What does Joshua 15:14 tell us that Caleb was, in fact, able to do?

12. Did Judah completely drive out the people of the land they inherited? (15:63)
            Yes   No

13. Did Ephraim completely drive out the people of the land they inherited? (16:10)
            Yes   No

14. Who was given credit for Manasseh receiving ten tracts of land? (17:3-6)

15. Did Manasseh completely drive out the people of the land they inherited? (17:12)
            Yes   No

---

[5] See the *Family of Israel* visual on p. 159

Week 6: An Unconquered Inheritance

16. At the end of Joshua Chapter 17, who approached Joshua requesting more land? (17:14, 17)

17. Mark up the *Boundaries of the Twelve Tribes* map on p.165 as follows:

    a. Use the key below to outline the boundary of each tribe.

Reubenites	Yellow
Gadites	Dark Pink
Half Tribe of Manasseh (East)	Light Blue
Judah	Purple
Ephraim	Dark Blue
Half Tribe of Manasseh (West)	Light Blue

    b. Circle in red the area of land given to Caleb. (15:13)

18. Summarize the primary focus of this section of Scripture in a single sentence.

Interpret

In this section, we will be studying to discover what the text <u>means</u>. These questions focus your attention on specific details, draw from other parts of the Bible to improve understanding, and highlight the bigger story of Scripture.

1. Review your highlights and underlines from the Read with Purpose section.

    a. Briefly summarize the Lord's activity:

    b. What characteristics of God did you notice? You can reference the list of attributes provided on pp. 160-161 for help.

2. As Chapter 13 opens, God told Joshua to distribute the land as an inheritance despite the fact that "a great deal of the land" remained unconquered.

    a. Look at the *Boundaries of the Twelve Tribes* map on p. 165. What observations do you have about the work that remained?

    b. How would distributing the unconquered lands motivate the people to persevere?

3. Joshua demonstrated godly leadership as he distributed the land as an inheritance. Fill in the *Godly Leadership* exhibit on p. 163 with information from this week's text.

Week 6: An Unconquered Inheritance

4. Besides Joshua, Caleb was the only person from the previous generation that God allowed to enter the Promised Land, and he was the first to receive an inheritance within Canaan.

   a. Compare the appeal Caleb made in this week's text (Joshua 14:6-12) to the appeal he made 45 years earlier in Numbers 14:2-9. What stands out to you from this?

   b. How can believers emulate Caleb's faith?

5. In an effort to motivate others to participate in the conquest of the land, Caleb offered his daughter Achsah in marriage to "whoever attacks and captures Kiriath-sepher." (15:16)

   a. Consider Achsah's reaction to this arrangement. Does this seem distressing to her? Why or why not?

   b. How might this proposal have been in the best interest of...

   Achsah?

   Othniel?

   Caleb?

   The entire tribe of Judah?

6. The Israelites' inheritance was based on God's promise to Abraham in Genesis 12:1-7.

    a. Read Hebrews 11:8. Note key information about Abraham and his inheritance.

    b. Similarly, believers do not yet fully know what we will receive as an inheritance from God. Read the following passages and note what we *do* know about it.

    1 Peter 1:3-5

    Ephesians 1:14

7. In Joshua Chapters 13-17, we saw several instances where the Israelites failed to drive out the inhabitants of the land.

    a. From the following passages, what did God warn would happen if the Israelites failed to drive out the inhabitants of the land?

    Numbers 33:50-55

    Exodus 23:33

    b. God had given the people an inheritance, yet in many instances, the Israelites did not fully take hold of it. The same can be true for believers today. Why do you think that is?

8. God had promised an inheritance to the Israelites. However, it was unconquered; they would have to act in order to receive it. This principle is seen throughout Scripture.

   a. Use the table below to note promises God previously made to the Israelites and what they had to do to receive those promises.

Passage	What did God promise?	What did the Israelites have to do?
Exodus 12:21-23		
Exodus 14:10-14		
Exodus 16:4		
Numbers 9:15-23		

   b. Just as the Israelites had to act, so must we. Note below promises God has made to believers and what we must do to receive them.

Passage	What does God promise?	What must believers do?
Matthew 11:28-30		
John 15:4-5		
James 1:12		
2 Peter 1:3-8		

Joshua   PURSUING THE PROMISES OF GOD

Apply

In this section, we'll consider ways in which God is speaking to us personally. The questions to the left focus on major themes and topics from this week of study. You can use those, or anything else the Lord brought to your attention, to answer the following:

God intervened when the people were delaying. What encouragement does this provide you regarding your own life?

God is the one that would drive out the enemy, but the people needed to act. Has God brought to mind any area where you need to act in order to receive victory?

Despite no guarantees, Caleb was bold in asking for a good, but difficult portion of land, reasoning "perhaps" the Lord would be with him. How does Caleb's faith encourage you? How does it challenge you?

Recognize His voice:
What did the Lord draw your attention to this week?

Respond to what He has said:
How can you respond?

Week 6: An Unconquered Inheritance

Final Thoughts
Use the space below to record any questions or takeaways you have regarding this week's material.

Repetitive Reading
It is of great benefit to repetitively read Scripture. Quickly read (or skim through) the entire book of Joshua at the end of each week of study. Record anything that stands out to you.

Pray
Think about what you have learned this week. Close by responding to the Lord in prayer.

LEAN IN

Notes from small group discussion:

LEARN

Notes from teaching session:

Every Promise Fulfilled

WEEK 7

Week 7: Every Promise Fulfilled

LISTEN

Pray
God is faithful; He keeps His promises. Begin your time of study in prayer. Spend some time recounting the ways in which God has been faithful to you. Ask Him to make you unwavering in your dependence upon Him.

> *Let us firmly hold the profession of our faith without wavering, for He who promised is faithful.*
> Hebrews 10:23 MEV

Reflect
From the past week of study, what had the most significant impact on you?

Read with Purpose
The Bible is primarily a book about God. As you read the passage of Scripture for Week 7 (Joshua Chapters 18-21), look first for what God says and does. Using the copy of the text on the pages that follow, *highlight in blue* everything God says, and *underline in blue* everything God does.

Note: This week's passage is fairly long. Your aim for Read with Purpose should be to read the text quickly, preferably in one sitting.

Joshua 18-21

LAND DISTRIBUTION AT SHILOH

18 The entire Israelite community assembled at Shiloh and set up the tent of meeting there. The land had been subdued before them, ² but seven tribes among the Israelites were left who had not divided up their inheritance. ³ So Joshua asked the Israelites, "How long will you delay going out to take possession of the land that the LORD, the God of your ancestors, gave you? ⁴ Appoint for yourselves three men from each tribe, and I will send them out. They are to go and survey the land, write a description of it for the purpose of their inheritance, and return to me. ⁵ Then they are to divide it into seven portions. Judah is to remain in its territory in the south and Joseph's family in their territory in the north. ⁶ When you have written a description of the seven portions of land and brought it to me, I will cast lots for you here in the presence of the LORD our God. ⁷ But the Levites among you do not get a portion, because their inheritance is the priesthood of the LORD. Gad, Reuben, and half the tribe of Manasseh have taken their inheritance beyond the Jordan to the east, which Moses the LORD's servant gave them."

⁸ As the men prepared to go, Joshua commanded them to write down a description of the land, saying, "Go and survey the land, write a description of it, and return to me. I will then cast lots for you here in Shiloh in the presence of the LORD." ⁹ So the men left, went through the land, and described it by towns in a document of seven sections. They returned to Joshua at the camp in Shiloh. ¹⁰ Joshua cast lots for them at Shiloh in the presence of the LORD where he distributed the land to the Israelites according to their divisions.

BENJAMIN'S INHERITANCE

¹¹ The lot came up for the tribe of Benjamin's descendants by their clans, and their allotted territory lay between Judah's descendants and Joseph's descendants.

¹² Their border on the north side began at the Jordan, ascended to the slope of Jericho on the north, through the hill country westward, and ended at the wilderness around Beth-aven. ¹³ From there the border went toward Luz, to the southern slope of Luz (that is, Bethel); it then went down by Ataroth-addar, over the hill south of Lower Beth-horon.

¹⁴ On the west side, from the hill facing Beth-horon on the south, the border curved, turning southward, and ended at Kiriath-baal (that is, Kiriath-jearim), a city of the descendants of Judah. This was the west side of their border.

¹⁵ The south side began at the edge of Kiriath-jearim, and the border extended westward; it went to the spring at the Waters of Nephtoah. ¹⁶ The border descended to the foot of the hill that faces Ben Hinnom Valley at the

northern end of Rephaim Valley. It ran down Hinnom Valley toward the south Jebusite slope and downward to En-rogel. ¹⁷ It curved northward and went to En-shemesh and on to Geliloth, which is opposite the Ascent of Adummim, and continued down to the Stone of Bohan son of Reuben. ¹⁸ Then it went north to the slope opposite the Arabah and proceeded into the plains. ¹⁹ The border continued to the north slope of Beth-hoglah and ended at the northern bay of the Dead Sea, at the southern end of the Jordan. This was the southern border.

²⁰ The Jordan formed the border on the east side.

This was the inheritance of Benjamin's descendants, by their clans, according to its surrounding borders.

BENJAMIN'S CITIES

²¹ These were the cities of the tribe of Benjamin's descendants by their clans:
Jericho, Beth-hoglah, Emek-keziz, ²² Beth-arabah, Zemaraim, Bethel, ²³ Avvim, Parah, Ophrah, ²⁴ Chephar-ammoni, Ophni, and Geba—twelve cities, with their settlements; ²⁵ Gibeon, Ramah, Beeroth, ²⁶ Mizpeh, Chephirah, Mozah, ²⁷ Rekem, Irpeel, Taralah, ²⁸ Zela, Haeleph, Jebus (that is, Jerusalem), Gibeah, and Kiriath—fourteen cities, with their settlements.

This was the inheritance for Benjamin's descendants by their clans.

SIMEON'S INHERITANCE

19 The second lot came out for Simeon, for the tribe of his descendants by their clans, but their inheritance was within the inheritance given to Judah's descendants.

² Their inheritance included
Beer-sheba (or Sheba), Moladah, ³ Hazar-shual, Balah, Ezem, ⁴ Eltolad, Bethul, Hormah, ⁵ Ziklag, Beth-marcaboth, Hazar-susah, ⁶ Beth-lebaoth, and Sharuhen—thirteen cities, with their settlements; ⁷ Ain, Rimmon, Ether, and Ashan—four cities, with their settlements; ⁸ and all the settlements surrounding these cities as far as Baalath-beer (Ramah in the south).

This was the inheritance of the tribe of Simeon's descendants by their clans. ⁹ The inheritance of Simeon's descendants was within the territory of Judah's descendants, because the share for Judah's descendants was too large. So Simeon's descendants received an inheritance within Judah's portion.

ZEBULUN'S INHERITANCE

¹⁰ The third lot came up for Zebulun's descendants by their clans.
The territory of their inheritance stretched as far as Sarid; ¹¹ their border went up westward to Maralah, reached Dabbesheth, and met the brook east of Jokneam. ¹² From Sarid, it turned due east along the border of Chisloth-tabor, went to Daberath, and went up to Japhia. ¹³ From there, it

went due east to Gath-hepher and to Eth-kazin; it extended to Rimmon, curving around to Neah. ¹⁴ The border then circled around Neah on the north to Hannathon and ended at Iphtah-el Valley, ¹⁵ along with Kattath, Nahalal, Shimron, Idalah, and Bethlehem—twelve cities, with their settlements.

¹⁶ This was the inheritance of Zebulun's descendants by their clans, these cities, with their settlements.

ISSACHAR'S INHERITANCE

¹⁷ The fourth lot came out for the tribe of Issachar's descendants by their clans. ¹⁸ Their territory went to Jezreel, and included Chesulloth, Shunem, ¹⁹ Hapharaim, Shion, Anaharath, ²⁰ Rabbith, Kishion, Ebez, ²¹ Remeth, En-gannim, En-haddah, and Beth-pazzez. ²² The border reached Tabor, Shahazumah, and Beth-shemesh, and ended at the Jordan—sixteen cities, with their settlements.

²³ This was the inheritance of the tribe of Issachar's descendants by their clans, the cities, with their settlements.

ASHER'S INHERITANCE

²⁴ The fifth lot came out for the tribe of Asher's descendants by their clans. ²⁵ Their boundary included Helkath, Hali, Beten, Achshaph, ²⁶ Allammelech, Amad, and Mishal and reached westward to Carmel and Shihor-libnath. ²⁷ It turned eastward to Beth-dagon, reached Zebulun and Iphtah-el Valley, north toward Beth-emek and Neiel, and went north to Cabul, ²⁸ Ebron, Rehob, Hammon, and Kanah, as far as greater Sidon. ²⁹ The boundary then turned to Ramah as far as the fortified city of Tyre; it turned back to Hosah and ended at the Mediterranean Sea, including Mahalab, Achzib, ³⁰ Ummah, Aphek, and Rehob—twenty-two cities, with their settlements.

³¹ This was the inheritance of the tribe of Asher's descendants by their clans, these cities with their settlements.

NAPHTALI'S INHERITANCE

³² The sixth lot came out for Naphtali's descendants by their clans. ³³ Their boundary went from Heleph and from the oak in Zaanannim, including Adami-nekeb and Jabneel, as far as Lakkum, and ended at the Jordan. ³⁴ To the west, the boundary turned to Aznoth-tabor and went from there to Hukkok, reaching Zebulun on the south, Asher on the west, and Judah at the Jordan on the east. ³⁵ The fortified cities were Ziddim, Zer, Hammath, Rakkath, Chinnereth, ³⁶ Adamah, Ramah, Hazor, ³⁷ Kedesh, Edrei, En-hazor, ³⁸ Iron, Migdal-el, Horem, Beth-anath, and Beth-shemesh—nineteen cities, with their settlements.

⁹⁹ This was the inheritance of the tribe of Naphtali's descendants by their clans, the cities with their settlements.

DAN'S INHERITANCE
⁴⁰ The seventh lot came out for the tribe of Dan's descendants by their clans. ⁴¹ The territory of their inheritance included Zorah, Eshtaol, Ir-shemesh, ⁴² Shaalabbin, Aijalon, Ithlah, ⁴³ Elon, Timnah, Ekron, ⁴⁴ Eltekeh, Gibbethon, Baalath, ⁴⁵ Jehud, Bene-berak, Gath-rimmon, ⁴⁶ Me-jarkon, and Rakkon, with the territory facing Joppa.
⁴⁷ When the territory of the descendants of Dan slipped out of their control, they went up and fought against Leshem, captured it, and struck it down with the sword. So they took possession of it, lived there, and renamed Leshem after their ancestor Dan. ⁴⁸ This was the inheritance of the tribe of Dan's descendants by their clans, these cities with their settlements.

JOSHUA'S INHERITANCE
⁴⁹ When they had finished distributing the land into its territories, the Israelites gave Joshua son of Nun an inheritance among them. ⁵⁰ By the LORD's command, they gave him the city Timnath-serah in the hill country of Ephraim, which he requested. He rebuilt the city and lived in it.
⁵¹ These were the portions that the priest Eleazar, Joshua son of Nun, and the family heads distributed to the Israelite tribes by lot at Shiloh in the LORD's presence at the entrance to the tent of meeting. So they finished dividing up the land.

CITIES OF REFUGE
20 Then the LORD spoke to Joshua, ² "Tell the Israelites: Select your cities of refuge, as I instructed you through Moses, ³ so that a person who kills someone unintentionally or accidentally may flee there. These will be your refuge from the avenger of blood. ⁴ When someone flees to one of these cities, stands at the entrance of the city gate, and states his case before the elders of that city, they are to bring him into the city and give him a place to live among them. ⁵ And if the avenger of blood pursues him, they must not hand the one who committed manslaughter over to him, for he killed his neighbor accidentally and did not hate him beforehand. ⁶ He is to stay in that city until he stands trial before the assembly and until the death of the high priest serving at that time. Then the one who committed manslaughter may return home to his own city from which he fled."
⁷ So they designated Kedesh in the hill country of Naphtali in Galilee, Shechem in the hill country of Ephraim, and Kiriath-arba (that is, Hebron) in the hill country of Judah. ⁸ Across the Jordan east of Jericho, they selected Bezer on the wilderness plateau from Reuben's tribe, Ramoth in Gilead from Gad's tribe,

and Golan in Bashan from Manasseh's tribe.
⁹ These are the cities appointed for all the Israelites and the aliens residing among them, so that anyone who kills a person unintentionally may flee there and not die at the hand of the avenger of blood until he stands before the assembly.

CITIES OF THE LEVITES

21 The Levite family heads approached the priest Eleazar, Joshua son of Nun, and the family heads of the Israelite tribes. ² At Shiloh, in the land of Canaan, they told them, "The LORD commanded through Moses that we be given cities to live in, with their pasturelands for our livestock." ³ So the Israelites, by the LORD's command, gave the Levites these cities with their pasturelands from their inheritance.

⁴ The lot came out for the Kohathite clans: The Levites who were the descendants of the priest Aaron received thirteen cities by lot from the tribes of Judah, Simeon, and Benjamin. ⁵ The remaining descendants of Kohath received ten cities by lot from the clans of the tribes of Ephraim, Dan, and half the tribe of Manasseh.

⁶ Gershon's descendants received thirteen cities by lot from the clans of the tribes of Issachar, Asher, Naphtali, and half the tribe of Manasseh in Bashan.

⁷ Merari's descendants received twelve cities for their clans from the tribes of Reuben, Gad, and Zebulun.

⁸ The Israelites gave these cities with their pasturelands around them to the Levites by lot, as the LORD had commanded through Moses.

CITIES OF AARON'S DESCENDANTS

⁹ The Israelites gave these cities by name from the tribes of the descendants of Judah and Simeon ¹⁰ to the descendants of Aaron from the Kohathite clans of the Levites, because they received the first lot. ¹¹ They gave them Kiriath-arba (that is, Hebron; Arba was the father of Anak) with its surrounding pasturelands in the hill country of Judah. ¹² But they gave the fields and settlements of the city to Caleb son of Jephunneh as his possession.

¹³ They gave to the descendants of the priest Aaron:

Hebron, the city of refuge for the one who commits manslaughter, with its pasturelands, Libnah with its pasturelands, ¹⁴ Jattir with its pasturelands, Eshtemoa with its pasturelands, ¹⁵ Holon with its pasturelands, Debir with its pasturelands, ¹⁶ Ain with its pasturelands, Juttah with its pasturelands, and Beth-shemesh with its pasturelands—nine cities from these two tribes.

¹⁷ From the tribe of Benjamin they gave:

Gibeon with its pasturelands, Geba with its pasturelands, ¹⁸ Anathoth with its pasturelands, and Almon with its pasturelands—four cities. ¹⁹ All thirteen cities with their pasturelands were for the priests, the descendants of Aaron.

CITIES OF KOHATH'S OTHER DESCENDANTS

20 The allotted cities to the remaining clans of Kohath's descendants, who were Levites, came from the tribe of Ephraim. 21 The Israelites gave them:

Shechem, the city of refuge for the one who commits manslaughter, with its pasturelands in the hill country of Ephraim, Gezer with its pasturelands, 22 Kibzaim with its pasturelands, and Beth-horon with its pasturelands—four cities.

23 From the tribe of Dan they gave:

Elteke with its pasturelands, Gibbethon with its pasturelands, 24 Aijalon with its pasturelands, and Gath-rimmon with its pasturelands—four cities.

25 From half the tribe of Manasseh they gave:

Taanach with its pasturelands and Gath-rimmon with its pasturelands—two cities.

26 All ten cities with their pasturelands were for the clans of Kohath's other descendants.

CITIES OF GERSHON'S DESCENDANTS

27 From half the tribe of Manasseh, they gave to the descendants of Gershon, who were one of the Levite clans:

Golan, the city of refuge for the one who commits manslaughter, with its pasturelands in Bashan, and Beeshterah with its pasturelands—two cities.

28 From the tribe of Issachar they gave:

Kishion with its pasturelands, Daberath with its pasturelands, 29 Jarmuth with its pasturelands, and En-gannim with its pasturelands—four cities.

30 From the tribe of Asher they gave:

Mishal with its pasturelands, Abdon with its pasturelands, 31 Helkath with its pasturelands, and Rehob with its pasturelands—four cities.

32 From the tribe of Naphtali they gave:

Kedesh in Galilee, the city of refuge for the one who commits manslaughter, with its pasturelands, Hammoth-dor with its pasturelands, and Kartan with its pasturelands—three cities.

33 All thirteen cities with their pasturelands were for the Gershonites by their clans.

CITIES OF MERARI'S DESCENDANTS

34 From the tribe of Zebulun, they gave to the clans of the descendants of Merari, who were the remaining Levites:

Jokneam with its pasturelands, Kartah with its pasturelands, 35 Dimnah with its pasturelands, and Nahalal with its pasturelands—four cities.

36 From the tribe of Reuben they gave:

Bezer with its pasturelands, Jahzah with its pasturelands, ³⁷ Kedemoth with its pasturelands, and Mephaath with its pasturelands—four cities.
³⁸ From the tribe of Gad they gave:
Ramoth in Gilead, the city of refuge for the one who commits manslaughter, with its pasturelands, Mahanaim with its pasturelands, ³⁹ Heshbon with its pasturelands, and Jazer with its pasturelands—four cities in all. ⁴⁰ All twelve cities were allotted to the clans of Merari's descendants, the remaining Levite clans.
⁴¹ Within the Israelite possession there were forty-eight cities in all with their pasturelands for the Levites. ⁴² Each of these cities had its own surrounding pasturelands; this was true for all the cities.

THE LORD'S PROMISES FULFILLED

⁴³ So the LORD gave Israel all the land he had sworn to give their ancestors, and they took possession of it and settled there. ⁴⁴ The LORD gave them rest on every side according to all he had sworn to their ancestors. None of their enemies were able to stand against them, for the LORD handed over all their enemies to them. ⁴⁵ None of the good promises the LORD had made to the house of Israel failed. Everything was fulfilled.

Week 7: Every Promise Fulfilled

Comprehend

In this section, we will examine closely what the Biblical text says. These questions are designed to help you notice and retain important details from this section of Scripture.

1. Joshua Chapter 18 begins with the entire Israelite community assembled at Shiloh. What did they set up there? (18:1)

2. Despite the fact that the land had been subdued, what had seven of the tribes not yet done? (18:2)

3. Joshua posed the Israelites with a question. Fill in the blanks from Joshua 18:3:

   How long will you _____ going out to _____ _____ of the land that the Lord, the God of your ancestors, gave you?

4. The Levites did not receive a portion of land for their inheritance. What *was* their inheritance? Use Joshua 18:7 to complete the block next to "Levi" on the *Family of Israel* visual on p. 159.

5. By what means did Joshua distribute the land to the Israelites? (18:10)

6. What was unique about the inheritance of the tribe of Simeon? (19:9)

7. The inheritance for the tribe of Dan was also unique. After losing control of the land they received by lot, they captured a completely different portion of land. See the *Boundaries of the Twelve Tribes* map on p.165.

    a. Outline Dan's original inheritance (the section near Judah) in dark green.

    b. Circle in dark green the area Dan later captured and claimed (near Naphtali).

111

8. Mark up the *Boundaries of the Twelve Tribes* map on p.165 as follows:

    a. Use the key below to outline the boundary of each tribe.

Benjamin	Teal
Zebulun	Orange
Issachar	Peach
Asher	Light Pink
Naphtali	Light Green

    b. Circle in red the area of land given to Joshua. (19:50)

9. When did Joshua receive his inheritance of land? (19:49)

10. Joshua Chapter 20 opens with the Lord speaking to Joshua.

    a. What did he remind the Israelites to do? (20:2)

    b. Why was this to be done? (20:3)

11. After whose death could the person who had killed someone unintentionally leave the city of refuge? (20:6)

12. Mark each city of refuge with an asterisk (*) on the *Boundaries of the Twelve Tribes* map on p.165. (20:7-8)

13. Besides the Israelites, who else could flee to a city of refuge after unintentionally killing someone? (20:9)

14. Although the Levites did not receive an inheritance of land, they did receive cities to live in and pasturelands for their livestock. By what means were these cities distributed to them? (21:8)

15. According to Joshua 21:9-40, which of the 12 tribes gave cities to the Levites? Circle all that apply.

Reuben	Simeon	Judah	Issachar
Zebulun	Gad	Asher	Dan
Naphtali	Manasseh	Ephraim	Benjamin

16. How many cities with their surrounding pasturelands were the Levites given in all? (21:41)

17. As Chapter 21 closes, we are told that "everything was fulfilled" of all the good promises the Lord made Israel. What two things had the Lord given them according to Joshua 21:43-44?

18. Summarize the primary focus of this section of Scripture in a single sentence.

Interpret

In this section, we will be studying to discover what the text <u>means</u>. These questions focus your attention on specific details, draw from other parts of the Bible to improve understanding, and highlight the bigger story of Scripture.

1. Review your highlights and underlines from the Read with Purpose section.

    a. Briefly summarize the Lord's activity:

    b. What characteristics of God did you notice? You can reference the list of attributes provided on pp. 160-161 for help.

2. In Joshua 18:1, we were told that the community set up the tent of meeting in the city of Shiloh. Read Deuteronomy 12:10-14.

    a. Who did Moses say would choose the place where the tent of meeting would be set up?

    b. What were the people to do in this place?

    c. What were they to be careful *not* to do?

3. This week, we were told that the land had been subdued (brought under control) by the Israelites.

    a. Although the land was subdued, the people were delaying to take possession of it. Why might this have been? List anything that comes to mind.

    b. What warning does this provide to believers?

Week 7: Every Promise Fulfilled

4. Joshua was unwavering as he exhorted the people to take possession of the land. Fill in the *Godly Leadership* exhibit on p. 163 with information from this week's text.

5. On his deathbed, the patriarch Jacob pronounced a prophecy regarding each of his sons. Simeon and Levi were given a joint prophecy, likely influenced by their extreme and violent actions avenging the rape of their sister Dinah in Genesis Chapter 34.

    a. Read Genesis 49:5-7. What did Jacob say would happen to their tribes?

    b. Look at the *Boundaries of the Twelve Tribes* map on p.165. Briefly note how we see Jacob's prophesy fulfilled.

6. Although Simeon and Levi received the same prophecy, the fulfillment of the prophecy for Levi's descendants took a more positive turn due to the tribe's subsequent actions.

    a. Read Exodus 32:19-29, which recounts the story of the golden calf. Here we see another act of violence by the Levites, but this time, in obedience to the Lord. Note the result of their obedience.

    b. What hope or encouragement does this provide believers?

7. Everyone received an inheritance. However, they did not all receive their inheritance in the same way.

   a. Use the table below to note how each person or group received their inheritance.

Group	How they received their inheritance
The Tribe of Reuben, Gad, and the ½ tribe of Manasseh (Manasseh East)	Numbers 32:1-5
Caleb	Joshua 14:6-12
Judah, Ephraim, Manasseh West, Benjamin, Simeon, Zebulun, Issachar, Asher, Naphtali	Joshua 14:1-2
Dan	Joshua 19:40-48
Joshua	Joshua 19:49-50

   b. How does this challenge your view of receiving spiritual things from God?

8. In addition to providing protection to anyone who unintentionally killed another, the cities of refuge served a greater purpose for the entire Israelite community.

   a. From Numbers 35:33-34, what would protecting innocent bloodshed prevent?

   b. The Levites were responsible for the cities of refuge and would serve as elders there. From Joshua 20:4-5, what was their main responsibility?

Week 7: Every Promise Fulfilled

9. The cities of refuge given to the Israelites point us to the greater refuge we have in Jesus Christ. (See Hebrews 6:17-20.)

   a. Read Romans 5:6-9. From what does Christ provide us refuge?

   b. How is the refuge of Christ superior to that of the cities of refuge?

10. This week, we were told that every promise of the Lord was fulfilled for the Israelites, as the Lord gave them rest on every side.

   a. The rest God provided through Joshua to the Israelites points to a greater rest for God's people. Read Hebrews 4:1-11 and summarize its message to believers:

   b. How does this encourage you? How does it challenge you?

Joshua PURSUING THE PROMISES OF GOD

Apply

In this section, we'll consider ways in which God is speaking to us personally. The questions to the left focus on major themes and topics from this week of study. You can use those, or anything else the Lord brought to your attention, to answer the following:

Has God brought to mind any area where you have become complacent or discouraged and stopped pursuing the things of God?

Do you have clarity regarding where God has placed you and what responsibilities He has given you? How can you be a better steward of these things?

God can be trusted to fulfill every promise He makes. What promises has He fulfilled for you personally?

God gave the Israelites rest. How has God prompted your spirit regarding rest?

Recognize His voice:
What did the Lord draw your attention to this week?

Respond to what He has said:
How can you respond?

Week 7: Every Promise Fulfilled

Final Thoughts
Use the space below to record any questions or takeaways you have regarding this week's material.

Repetitive Reading
It is of great benefit to repetitively read Scripture. Quickly read (or skim through) the entire book of Joshua at the end of each week of study. Record anything that stands out to you.

Pray
Think about what you have learned this week. Close by responding to the Lord in prayer.

LEAN IN

Notes from small group discussion:

Week 7: Every Promise Fulfilled

LEARN

Notes from teaching session:

A Witness Between Us

WEEK 8

Week 8: A Witness Between Us

LISTEN

Pray
God is faithful; He cares about both the holiness of His people and peace amongst them. Come to God in humble prayer. Ask Him to use this week's passage to teach you how to better pursue both personal holiness and unity with others.

> *Pursue peace with everyone, and holiness–without it no one will see the Lord.*
> *Hebrews 12:14*

Reflect
From the past week of study, what had the most significant impact on you?

Read with Purpose
The Bible is primarily a book about God. As you read the passage of Scripture for Week 8 (Joshua Chapter 22), look for what the people of Israel think or know about God. Using the copy of the text on the pages that follow, *underline in green* any words or phrases the Israelites use to describe God or His actions.

Joshua 22

EASTERN TRIBES RETURN HOME

22 Joshua summoned the Reubenites, Gadites, and half the tribe of Manasseh ² and told them, "You have done everything Moses the LORD's servant commanded you and have obeyed me in everything I commanded you. ³ You have not deserted your brothers even once this whole time but have carried out the requirement of the command of the LORD your God. ⁴ Now that he has given your brothers rest, just as he promised them, return to your homes in your own land that Moses the LORD's servant gave you across the Jordan. ⁵ Only carefully obey the command and instruction that Moses the LORD's servant gave you: to love the LORD your God, walk in all his ways, keep his commands, be loyal to him, and serve him with all your heart and all your soul."

⁶ Joshua blessed them and sent them on their way, and they went to their homes. ⁷ Moses had given territory to half the tribe of Manasseh in Bashan, but Joshua had given territory to the other half, with their brothers, on the west side of the Jordan. When Joshua sent them to their homes and blessed them, ⁸ he said, "Return to your homes with great wealth: a huge number of cattle, and silver, gold, bronze, iron, and a large quantity of clothing. Share the spoil of your enemies with your brothers."

EASTERN TRIBES BUILD AN ALTAR

⁹ The Reubenites, Gadites, and half the tribe of Manasseh left the Israelites at Shiloh in the land of Canaan to return to their own land of Gilead, which they took possession of according to the LORD's command through Moses. ¹⁰ When they came to the region of the Jordan in the land of Canaan, the Reubenites, Gadites, and half the tribe of Manasseh built a large, impressive altar there by the Jordan. ¹¹ Then the Israelites heard it said, "Look, the Reubenites, Gadites, and half the tribe of Manasseh have built an altar on the frontier of the land of Canaan at the region of the Jordan, on the Israelite side." ¹² When the Israelites heard this, the entire Israelite community assembled at Shiloh to go to war against them.

EXPLANATION OF THE ALTAR

¹³ The Israelites sent Phinehas son of Eleazar the priest to the Reubenites, Gadites, and half the tribe of Manasseh, in the land of Gilead. ¹⁴ They sent ten leaders with him—one family leader for each tribe of Israel. All of them were heads of their ancestral families among the clans of Israel. ¹⁵ They went to the Reubenites, Gadites, and half the tribe of Manasseh, in the land of Gilead, and told them, ¹⁶ "This is what the LORD's entire community says: 'What is this treachery you have committed today against the God of Israel by turning away from the LORD and building an altar for yourselves, so that you are in rebellion against the LORD today? ¹⁷ Wasn't the iniquity of Peor, which brought a plague on the LORD's community, enough for us? We have not cleansed ourselves from it even to this day, ¹⁸ and now would you turn away from the LORD? If you rebel against the LORD

today, tomorrow he will be angry with the entire community of Israel. ¹⁹ But if the land you possess is defiled, cross over to the land the LORD possesses where the LORD's tabernacle stands, and take possession of it among us. But don't rebel against the LORD or against us by building for yourselves an altar other than the altar of the LORD our God. ²⁰ Wasn't Achan son of Zerah unfaithful regarding what was set apart for destruction, bringing wrath on the entire community of Israel? He was not the only one who perished because of his iniquity.'"

²¹ The Reubenites, Gadites, and half the tribe of Manasseh answered the heads of the Israelite clans, ²² "The Mighty One, God, the LORD! The Mighty One, God, the LORD! He knows, and may Israel also know. Do not spare us today, if it was in rebellion or treachery against the LORD ²³ that we have built for ourselves an altar to turn away from him. May the LORD himself hold us accountable if we intended to offer burnt offerings and grain offerings on it, or to sacrifice fellowship offerings on it. ²⁴ We actually did this from a specific concern that in the future your descendants might say to our descendants, 'What relationship do you have with the LORD, the God of Israel? ²⁵ For the LORD has made the Jordan a border between us and you descendants of Reuben and Gad. You have no share in the LORD!' So your descendants may cause our descendants to stop fearing the LORD.

²⁶ "Therefore we said: Let's take action and build an altar for ourselves, but not for burnt offering or sacrifice. ²⁷ Instead, it is to be a witness between us and you, and between the generations after us, so that we may carry out the worship of the LORD in his presence with our burnt offerings, sacrifices, and fellowship offerings. Then in the future, your descendants will not be able to say to our descendants, 'You have no share in the LORD!' ²⁸ We thought that if they said this to us or to our generations in the future, we would reply: Look at the replica of the LORD's altar that our ancestors made, not for burnt offering or sacrifice, but as a witness between us and you. ²⁹ We would never ever rebel against the LORD or turn away from him today by building an altar for burnt offering, grain offering, or sacrifice, other than the altar of the LORD our God, which is in front of his tabernacle.

CONFLICT RESOLVED

³⁰ When the priest Phinehas and the community leaders, the heads of Israel's clans who were with him, heard what the descendants of Reuben, Gad, and Manasseh had to say, they were pleased. ³¹ Phinehas son of Eleazar the priest said to the descendants of Reuben, Gad, and Manasseh, "Today we know that the LORD is among us, because you have not committed this treachery against him. As a result, you have rescued the Israelites from the LORD's power."

³² Then the priest Phinehas son of Eleazar and the leaders returned from the Reubenites and Gadites in the land of Gilead to the Israelites in the land of Canaan and brought back a report to them. ³³ The Israelites were pleased with the report, and they blessed God. They spoke no more about going to war against them to ravage the land where the Reubenites and Gadites lived. ³⁴ So the Reubenites and Gadites named the altar: It is a witness between us that the LORD is God.

Comprehend

In this section, we will examine closely what the Biblical text says. These questions are designed to help you notice and retain important details from this section of Scripture.

1. Joshua Chapter 22 begins with Joshua summoning the Reubenites, Gadites and half the tribe of Manasseh.

    a. What had they done? (22:2-3)

    b. What had they *not* done? (22:3)

    c. What could they now do? (22:4)

2. Joshua instructed the two and a half tribes to "carefully obey the command and instruction" that Moses had given them. What was that instruction? Use Joshua 22:5 to fill in the blanks:

    to _____ the LORD your God,

    _____ in all his ways,

    keep his _____,

    be _____ to him,

    and _____ him with all your _____ and all your _____.

3. Joshua sent the two and a half tribes to their homes with great wealth.

    a. Where did it come from? (22:8)

    b. What were they to do with it? (22:8)

4. As the Reubenites, Gadites, and half the tribe of Manasseh returned to their land, what did they build? (22:10)

5. How did the other Israelites react when they heard what the two and a half tribes had done? (22:12)

Week 8: A Witness Between Us

6. Who did the Israelites send to confront the Reubenites, Gadites and half the tribe of Manasseh? (22:13-14)

7. From Joshua 22:16, list the words the Israelites used to characterize what the two and a half tribes had done by building the altar.

8. What did they say would happen if the two and a half tribes rebelled against the Lord? (22:18)

9. What did Phinehas and the leaders invite the two and a half tribes to do *instead* of rebelling against the Lord? (22:19)

10. What reason did the Reubenites, Gadites, and half the tribe of Manasseh give for building the altar? (22:24-25)

11. From Joshua 22:26-27:

    a. What did they say the altar was *not* built for?

    b. What did they say the altar *was* built for?

12. What did the Reubenites, Gadites, and half the tribe of Manasseh proclaim to Phinehas in Joshua 22:29?

13. Were the Israelites satisfied by this response? (22:30-33)

    Yes   No

14. What did the Reubenites and Gadites name the altar they built? (22:34)

15. Summarize the primary focus of this section of Scripture in a single sentence.

Interpret

In this section, we will be studying to discover what the text means. These questions focus your attention on specific details, draw from other parts of the Bible to improve understanding, and highlight the bigger story of Scripture.

1. Review your underlines from the Read with Purpose section.

    a. Note attributes of God recognized by the Israelites (either directly or indirectly) in this week's Scripture. You can reference the list of attributes provided on pp. 160-161 for help.

    b. How did the Israelites' understanding of God impact their actions in this week's text?

2. After praising the eastern tribes for their exemplary faithfulness to the commitment they made many years earlier, Joshua sent them home, exhorting them to carefully obey the Lord.

    a. Read the words of Jesus in John 14:15. What does obedience to God demonstrate?

    b. What do the following passages say will result from obedience to God?

    Deuteronomy 12:28

    Deuteronomy 28:9

    John 15:10

3. The eastern tribes were concerned that being geographically separated from the rest of Israel would result in them gradually falling away from the other tribes and even God Himself.

   a. This was a valid concern. List reasons why:

   b. Careful obedience to God's commands given to all Israel would safeguard against these concerns. Use the passages below to note how:

Concern	Safeguard
That the western tribes would question the validity of the eastern tribes' relationship with God	Deuteronomy 16:16
That their descendants would eventually stop fearing the Lord	Deuteronomy 6:4-9

4. The building of the altar caused the western tribes to believe that the eastern tribes had committed idolatry. Read Deuteronomy 13:12-18.

   a. How had the western tribes acted consistently with what Moses had commanded them regarding idolatry?

   b. How does this passage help you understand Joshua 22:12 and 22:33?

5. In their confrontation, the leaders mentioned two previous instances of unfaithfulness that were disastrous for the Israelites. First, they mention the iniquity of Peor. Read Numbers 25:1-13.

   a. Briefly summarize what had happened at Peor:

   b. Consider Phinehas' actions at Peor. Why might he have been selected to lead the delegation to confront the eastern tribes?

6. The second instance of unfaithfulness the leaders referenced was that of Achan, whose disobedience caused the Israelites' defeat at Ai.

   a. The tribes claimed that Achan was not the only one who perished because of his iniquity. Who else died as a result of his actions? (See Joshua 7:5 and 7:24-26)

   b. Read the following passages. Why should believers be concerned about the actions of other believers?

   1 Corinthians 12:26

   Hebrews 12:15

   Ephesians 4:11-16

Week 8: A Witness Between Us

7. The eastern tribes were adamant - not only had they *not* entered into idolatry (the worship of another god), they also had no intention of worshiping God in ways He had not approved.

    a. Despite their best intentions, their actions were and could continue to be misunderstood. What future temptation might the replica altar pose?

    b. What lessons can believers take from this account?

8. The western tribes had a very strong reaction to what they rightly saw as a very serious offense.

    a. What might have resulted if the western tribes had avoided conflict with the eastern tribes instead of confronting it? List anything you can think of.

    b. Sometimes strong responses are necessary. Sometimes soft encouragement is the better approach. How can believers discern which approach to use?

9. Joshua demonstrated godly leadership as he sent the eastern tribes home. Fill in the *Godly Leadership* exhibit on p. 163 with information from this week's text.

10. This week, God's people boldly confronted their brothers regarding perceived rebellion against God. Their actions stand as a witness to us today.

    a. What wisdom do you see in how the Israelites confronted the Reubenites, Gadites, and the half tribe of Manasseh?

    b. What wisdom do you see in the response of the Reubenites, Gadites, and the half tribe of Manasseh?

    c. What takeaways do you have from this account?

Week 8: A Witness Between Us

Apply

In this section, we'll consider ways in which God is speaking to us personally. The questions to the left focus on major themes and topics from this week of study. You can use those, or anything else the Lord brought to your attention, to answer the following:

The eastern tribes were faithful to their commitment for years. Is God prompting you to work toward better follow through on commitments you make?

Has God drawn your attention to any of the following regarding conflict management in your own life:

-To more thoroughly investigate before jumping to conclusions?
-To address issues instead of avoiding them?
-To try a softer approach to confrontation?

How can you better pursue personal holiness? Unity with other believers?

Recognize His voice:
What did the Lord draw your attention to this week?

Respond to what He has said:
How can you respond?

Week 8: A Witness Between Us

Final Thoughts
Use the space below to record any questions or takeaways you have regarding this week's material.

Repetitive Reading
It is of great benefit to repetitively read Scripture. Quickly read (or skim through) the entire book of Joshua at the end of each week of study. Record anything that stands out to you.

Pray
Think about what you have learned this week. Close by responding to the Lord in prayer.

LEAN IN

Notes from small group discussion:

LEARN

Notes from teaching session:

Choose for Yourselves Today

WEEK 9

Week 9: Choose for Yourselves Today

LISTEN

Pray
God is faithful; He desires wholehearted devotion from those who follow Him. Begin your time of study in prayer. Ask God to reveal to you any places where you are divided in your loyalty to Him. Confess to Him your desire to follow Him fully.

> *And Jesus answered him, "It is written: Worship the Lord your God, and serve him only."*
> Luke 4:8

Reflect
From the past week of study, what had the most significant impact on you?

Read with Purpose
The Bible is primarily a book about God. As you read the passage of Scripture for Week 9 (Joshua Chapters 23-24), look first for what God says and does. Using the copy of the text on the pages that follow, *highlight in blue* everything God says, and *underline in blue* everything God does.

Joshua 23-24

JOSHUA'S FAREWELL ADDRESS

23 A long time after the LORD had given Israel rest from all the enemies around them, Joshua was old, advanced in age. ² So Joshua summoned all Israel, including its elders, leaders, judges, and officers, and said to them, "I am old, advanced in age, ³ and you have seen for yourselves everything the LORD your God did to all these nations on your account, because it was the LORD your God who was fighting for you. ⁴ See, I have allotted these remaining nations to you as an inheritance for your tribes, including all the nations I have destroyed, from the Jordan westward to the Mediterranean Sea. ⁵ The LORD your God will force them back on your account and drive them out before you so that you can take possession of their land, as the LORD your God promised you.

⁶ "Be very strong and continue obeying all that is written in the book of the law of Moses, so that you do not turn from it to the right or left ⁷ and so that you do not associate with these nations remaining among you. Do not call on the names of their gods or make an oath to them; do not serve them or bow in worship to them. ⁸ Instead, be loyal to the LORD your God, as you have been to this day.

⁹ "The LORD has driven out great and powerful nations before you, and no one is able to stand against you to this day. ¹⁰ One of you routed a thousand because the LORD your God was fighting for you, as he promised. ¹¹ So diligently watch yourselves! Love the LORD your God! ¹² If you ever turn away and become loyal to the rest of these nations remaining among you, and if you intermarry or associate with them and they with you, ¹³ know for certain that the LORD your God will not continue to drive these nations out before you. They will become a snare and a trap for you, a sharp stick for your sides and thorns in your eyes, until you disappear from this good land the LORD your God has given you.

¹⁴ "I am now going the way of the whole earth, and you know with all your heart and all your soul that none of the good promises the LORD your God made to you has failed. Everything was fulfilled for you; not one promise has failed. ¹⁵ Since every good thing the LORD your God promised you has come about, so he will bring on you every bad thing until he has annihilated you from this good land the LORD your God has given you. ¹⁶ If you break the covenant of the LORD your God, which he commanded you, and go and serve other gods, and bow in worship to them, the LORD's anger will burn against you, and you will quickly disappear from this good land he has given you."

REVIEW OF ISRAEL'S HISTORY

24 Joshua assembled all the tribes of Israel at Shechem and summoned Israel's elders, leaders, judges, and officers, and they presented themselves before God. ² Joshua said to all the people, "This is what the LORD, the God of Israel, says: 'Long ago your ancestors, including Terah, the father of Abraham and Nahor, lived beyond the Euphrates River and worshiped other gods. ³ But I took your father Abraham from the region beyond the Euphrates River, led him throughout the land of Canaan, and multiplied his descendants. I gave him Isaac, ⁴ and to Isaac I gave Jacob and Esau. I gave the hill country of Seir to Esau as a possession.

"'Jacob and his sons, however, went down to Egypt. ⁵ I sent Moses and Aaron, and I defeated Egypt by what I did within it, and afterward I brought you out. ⁶ When I brought your ancestors out of Egypt and you reached the Red Sea, the Egyptians pursued your ancestors with chariots and horsemen as far as the sea. ⁷ Your ancestors cried out to the LORD, so he put darkness between you and the Egyptians, and brought the sea over them, engulfing them. Your own eyes saw what I did to Egypt. After that, you lived in the wilderness a long time. ⁸ "'Later, I brought you to the land of the Amorites who lived beyond the Jordan. They fought against you, but I handed them over to you. You possessed their land, and I annihilated them before you. ⁹ Balak son of Zippor, king of Moab, set out to fight against Israel. He sent for Balaam son of Beor to curse you, ¹⁰ but I would not listen to Balaam. Instead, he repeatedly blessed you, and I rescued you from him.

¹¹ "'You then crossed the Jordan and came to Jericho. Jericho's citizens—as well as the Amorites, Perizzites, Canaanites, Hethites, Girgashites, Hivites, and Jebusites—fought against you, but I handed them over to you. ¹² I sent hornets ahead of you, and they drove out the two Amorite kings before you. It was not by your sword or bow. ¹³ I gave you a land you did not labor for, and cities you did not build, though you live in them; you are eating from vineyards and olive groves you did not plant.'

THE COVENANT RENEWAL

¹⁴ "Therefore, fear the LORD and worship him in sincerity and truth. Get rid of the gods your ancestors worshiped beyond the Euphrates River and in Egypt, and worship the LORD. ¹⁵ But if it doesn't please you to worship the LORD, choose for yourselves today: Which will you worship—the gods your ancestors worshiped beyond the Euphrates River or the gods of the Amorites in whose land you are living? As for me and my family, we will worship the LORD."

¹⁶ The people replied, "We will certainly not abandon the LORD to worship other gods! ¹⁷ For the LORD our God brought us and our ancestors out of the land of Egypt, out of the place of slavery, and performed these great signs before our eyes. He also protected us all along the way we went and among all the peoples whose lands we traveled through. ¹⁸ The LORD drove out before us all the peoples, including the Amorites who lived in the land. We too will worship the LORD, because he is our God."

¹⁹ But Joshua told the people, "You will not be able to worship the LORD, because he is a holy God. He is a jealous God; he will not forgive your transgressions and sins. ²⁰ If you abandon the LORD and worship foreign gods, he will turn against you, harm you, and completely destroy you, after he has been good to you."

²¹ "No!" the people answered Joshua. "We will worship the LORD."
²² Joshua then told the people, "You are witnesses against yourselves that you yourselves have chosen to worship the LORD."
"We are witnesses," they said.
²³ "Then get rid of the foreign gods that are among you and turn your hearts to the LORD, the God of Israel."
²⁴ So the people said to Joshua, "We will worship the LORD our God and obey him."
²⁵ On that day Joshua made a covenant for the people at Shechem and established a statute and ordinance for them. ²⁶ Joshua recorded these things in the book of the law of God; he also took a large stone and set it up there under the oak at the sanctuary of the LORD. ²⁷ And Joshua said to all the people, "You see this stone—it will be a witness against us, for it has heard all the words the LORD said to us, and it will be a witness against you, so that you will not deny your God." ²⁸ Then Joshua sent the people away, each to his own inheritance.

BURIAL OF THREE LEADERS

²⁹ After these things, the LORD's servant, Joshua son of Nun, died at the age of 110. ³⁰ They buried him in his allotted territory at Timnath-serah, in the hill country of Ephraim north of Mount Gaash. ³¹ Israel worshiped the LORD throughout Joshua's lifetime and during the lifetimes of the elders who outlived Joshua and who had experienced all the works the LORD had done for Israel.

³² Joseph's bones, which the Israelites had brought up from Egypt, were buried at Shechem in the parcel of land Jacob had purchased from the sons of Hamor, Shechem's father, for a hundred pieces of silver. It was an inheritance for Joseph's descendants.

³³ And Eleazar son of Aaron died, and they buried him at Gibeah, which had been given to his son Phinehas in the hill country of Ephraim.

Comprehend

In this section, we will examine closely what the Biblical text says. These questions are designed to help you notice and retain important details from this section of Scripture.

1. According to Joshua 23:1, when did Joshua summon all Israel to deliver his farewell address?

2. What did Joshua say the people had seen for themselves? (23:3)

3. God would continue to force back the remaining nations. According to Joshua 23:5, why would He do this?

4. Read Joshua 23:6-11. List below everything Joshua told the people *to do* and *not* to do:

Do	Do not do

5. What, according to Joshua 23:14, did the Israelites know with all their heart and soul?

6. What did Joshua say would happen if the people turned away from God and broke their covenant with him? (23:13, 15-16)

7. As Chapter 24 opens, where did Joshua have the tribes, elders, leaders, judges and officers assemble? (24:1)

8. Before listing a number of actions He took on their behalf, what did God remind the Israelites that their ancestors had done? (24:2)

9. Fill in the blanks below, listing some of the actions the Lord had taken on behalf of Israel.

   I _____ your father Abraham from the region beyond the Euphrates River, _____ him through the land of Canaan, and _____ his descendants. (24:3)

   I _____ him Isaac (24:3), and to Isaac I _____ Jacob and Esau. (24:4)

   I _____ Moses and Aaron, (24:5)

   I _____ Egypt by what I did within it, and afterward I _____ you out. (24:5)

   I _____ you to the land of the Amorites (24:8)

   I _____ them over to you. (24:8)

   I _____ them before you. (24:8)

   I _____ you from him (Balaam). (24:10)

   I _____ hornets ahead of you, (24:12)

   I _____ you a land you did not labor for, and cities you did not build, (24:13)

10. What three things does Joshua tell the people to do as a result of all the Lord had done for them? (24:14)

11. What choice did Joshua place before the Israelites? (24:15)

12. How did the people respond? (24:16-18)

Week 9: Choose for Yourselves Today

13. Joshua issued a warning to the Israelites. What was it? (24:20)

14. What two things did Joshua tell the people to do? (24:23)

15. Before sending the people away to their own inheritance, Joshua set up a stone as a witness. Why did he do this? (24:27)

16. As the book of Joshua ends, we are given details of the burials of three of Israel's leaders. Who were they?

17. What is noted about how long the Israelites worshiped the Lord? (24:31)

18. Summarize the primary focus of this section of Scripture in a single sentence.

Interpret

In this section, we will be studying to discover what the text means. These questions focus your attention on specific details, draw from other parts of the Bible to improve understanding, and highlight the bigger story of Scripture.

1. Review your highlights and underlines from the Read with Purpose section.

    a. Briefly summarize the Lord's activity:

    b. What characteristics of God did you notice? You can reference the list of attributes provided on pp. 160-161 for help.

2. In his farewell address, Joshua began by reminding the Israelites that God would continue to force their enemies back, *if* they remained loyal to Him.

    a. The process of driving out their enemies was long. How would the length of this process test their loyalty to God?

    b. How do we see this principle at play in the spiritual development of believers?

3. The Israelites would need to be "very strong" in order to continue obeying God and stay loyal to Him. Why do believers today also need to be "very strong" in order to do these same things?

Week 9: Choose for Yourselves Today

4. Joshua urged the Israelites to "diligently watch" themselves. Consider how the following disciplines help believers ensure we are focused on God and His priorities.

   Remembrance:

   Time in the word:

   Prayer:

   Biblical community:

   Serving God:

   Sabbath (Rest):

5. As Chapter 24 opens, Joshua assembled the leaders of Israel at Shechem, a city with great significance to the Israelites.

   a. Note from the following passages significant events that had previously happened at Shechem.

Passage	What had happened previously in Shechem?
Genesis 12:1-7	
Genesis 35:1-5	

   b. Why might Joshua have chosen this place for the covenant renewal?

6. After reminding the people of all that God had done for them, Joshua turned his attention to worship. What further instruction do the following passages provide regarding worship that is pleasing to God?

   Psalm 96:2-9

   Romans 12:1-8

   1 Peter 4:10-11

7. Joshua warned the Israelites, "If you abandon the Lord and worship foreign gods, he will turn against you, harm you, and completely destroy you, after he has been good to you."

   a. Read the following passages, which contain similar messages. Use the table below to note what warnings and assurances they provide:

Passage	Warning	Assurances
2 Chronicles 15:2		
Ezekiel 18:26-32		
Romans 11:20-23		

   b. Do these passages challenge your current thinking? If so, how?

8. Joshua wholeheartedly served the Lord and His people all the days of his life. Fill in the *Godly Leadership* exhibit on p. 163 with information from this week's text.

9. Throughout Chapters 23-24, Joshua warned of the dangers of idolatry, abandoning loyalty to God by worshiping and serving other gods.

   a. Idolatry remains a great danger to believers. Choose a few of the modern day "idols" listed below. Make note of what it might look like to worship or serve them.

Idol	Worship	Serve
Productivity		
Perfectionism		
Consumerism		
Comfort / Pleasure		
Success / Notoriety		
Politics		
Convenience		

   b. Anything can become an idol if we trust it more than God, or if it becomes our highest priority. How can believers safeguard against turning God-given resources into idols?

   c. The Israelites were oblivious that they were doing the very thing Joshua was warning about. How should this impact believers?

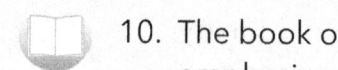

10. The book of Joshua shows God to be faithful to keep His promises and emphasizes the importance of our faithfulness to Him.

    a. Joshua told God's people who had *already* chosen Him, to "choose for yourselves today." Read Luke 9:23. What similar message did Jesus give?

    b. Practically speaking, what might this daily choice look like in the life of a believer?

Week 9: Choose for Yourselves Today

Joshua   PURSUING THE PROMISES OF GOD

Apply

In this section, we'll consider ways in which God is speaking to us personally. The questions to the left focus on major themes and topics from this week of study. You can use those, or anything else the Lord brought to your attention, to answer the following:

God moved mightily on behalf of the Israelites. List some ways He has moved mightily in your life.

How has this week's passage challenged your view of idolatry?
-Which "gods" of your parents might you be prone to prioritize?
-Which "gods" of your city or country might you be prone to prioritize?

How can you diligently watch yourself? Turn your heart consistently to the Lord?

Has God brought to mind ways you personally can choose for yourself daily to follow Him?

Recognize His voice:
What did the Lord draw your attention to this week?

Respond to what He has said:
How can you respond?

Week 9: Choose for Yourselves Today

Final Thoughts
Use the space below to record any questions or takeaways you have regarding this week's material.

Repetitive Reading
It is of great benefit to repetitively read Scripture. Quickly read (or skim through) the entire book of Joshua at the end of each week of study. Record anything that stands out to you.

Pray
Think about what you have learned this week. Close by responding to the Lord in prayer.

LEAN IN

Notes from small group discussion:

Week 9: Choose for Yourselves Today

LEARN

Notes from teaching session:

Study Reflection

JOSHUA

Study Reflection

Before you close this study of the book of Joshua, take time to note how God has worked in you through the words of this specific book of the Bible.

Pray
Begin this time in prayer. Thank the Lord for His word and all that He has revealed through it during this time of study.

Reflect
Review your answers to the Interpret and Apply questions for Weeks 2-9. Note things you'd like to remember from this study.

Apply
What are some specific ways you can apply the truths from Joshua to your life?

Supplemental Materials

The Family of Israel

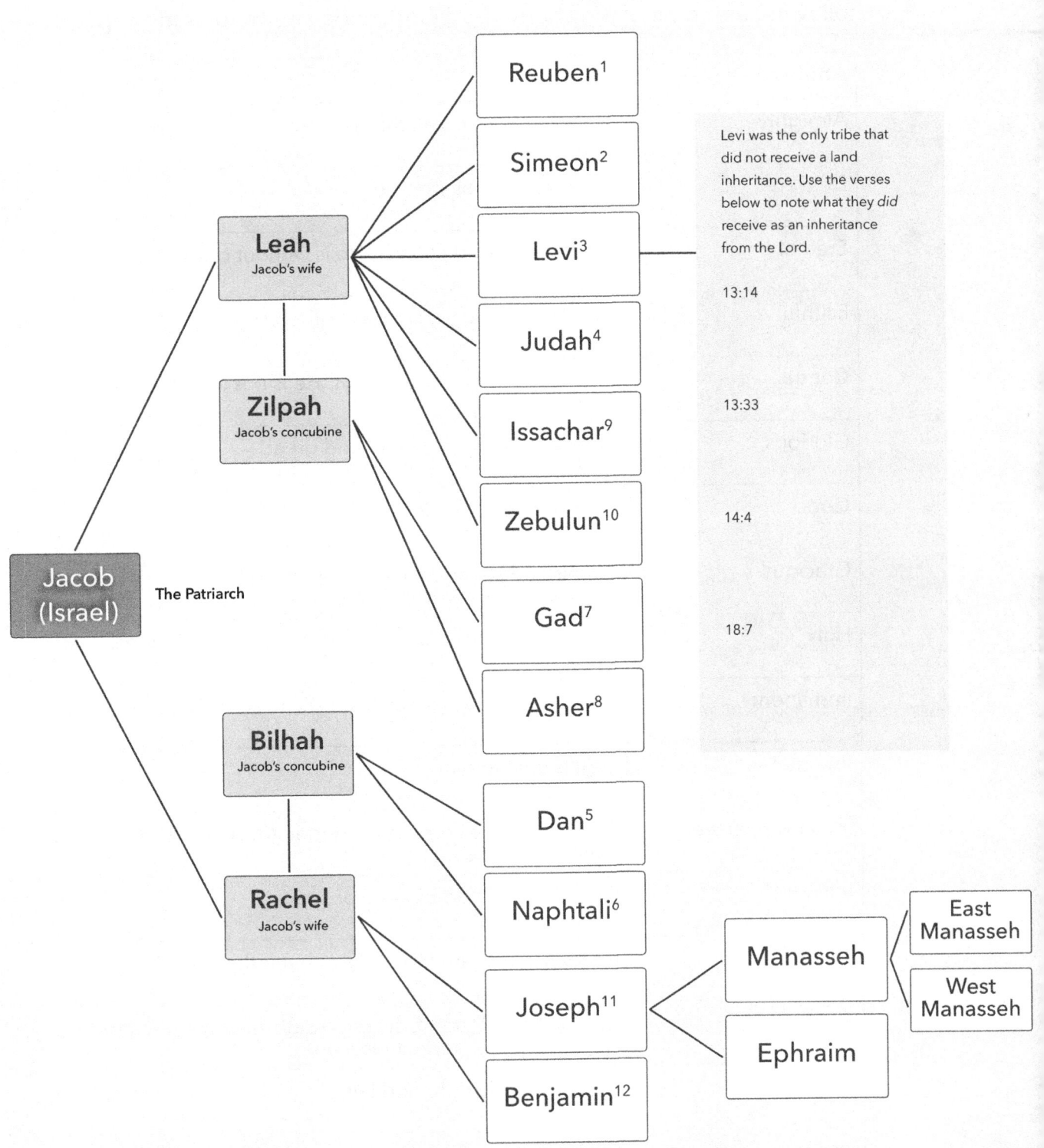

- **Jacob (Israel)** — The Patriarch
  - **Leah** (Jacob's wife)
    - Reuben[1]
    - Simeon[2]
    - Levi[3]
    - Judah[4]
    - Issachar[9]
    - Zebulun[10]
  - **Zilpah** (Jacob's concubine)
    - Gad[7]
    - Asher[8]
  - **Bilhah** (Jacob's concubine)
    - Dan[5]
    - Naphtali[6]
  - **Rachel** (Jacob's wife)
    - Joseph[11]
      - Manasseh
        - East Manasseh
        - West Manasseh
      - Ephraim
    - Benjamin[12]

Levi was the only tribe that did not receive a land inheritance. Use the verses below to note what they *did* receive as an inheritance from the Lord.

13:14

13:33

14:4

18:7

Note: The number next to each name indicates the birth order of Jacob's sons.

159

Attributes of God

God reveals His nature and character through the pages of Scripture. The following are some of the attributes of God made known to us in Scripture.

Attribute	Meaning
Almighty	God is able to do all things.
Deliverer	God rescues His people.
Eternal	God has existed forever; He is without origin.
Faithful	God does what He says He will do.
Gentle	God is of kind temperament; He is not unduly harsh or severe.
Glorious	God is infinitely beautiful and great.
Good	God does what is right.
Gracious	God is compassionate; He is inclined to show His people kindness and favor.
Holy	God is perfect; He is set-apart from all other things.
Immanent	God is near; He is involved in the lives of His people.
Immutable	God is unchanging.
Incomprehensible	God cannot be completely understood or fully explained by finite human beings.
Infinite	God is not limited by time or space.
Jealous	God will not share His glory with another.
Judge	God is the final authority regarding what is right and wrong; He administers perfect justice.
Just	God is morally right and fair.
Loving	God feels and shows great care for His people.

Attribute	Meaning
Merciful	God is inclined to grant forgiveness and pardon sin.
Miraculous	God is supernatural; He has no limitations.
Omnipotent	God is all-powerful.
Omnipresent	God is everywhere.
Omniscient	God is all-knowing.
Paternal	God is a father to His people.
Patient	God is slow to anger and long-suffering.
Protector	God protects and defends His people.
Providential	God exercises divine guidance over the affairs of humanity for the purpose of His sovereign will.
Provider	God provides everything His people need.
Redeemer	God is the one who pays the price to set His people free.
Righteous	God is blameless.
Savior	God is the one who brings salvation.
Self-Existent	God was not created; He exists independently of all other beings.
Self-Sufficient	God has no needs.
Sovereign	God is in control; He acts on behalf of His will.
Transcendent	God exists apart from, and is not subject to, the limitations of the material universe.
Trustworthy	God is dependable; He is worthy of our complete confidence.
Truthful	God is honest; He cannot lie.
Wise	God has all knowledge and understands everything; He gives perfect direction and guidance.

Godly Leadership

Called to Lead, Chapters 1-2

Godly leaders have been prepared for the task ahead of them, have demonstrated they can be trusted and have assurance of their calling.

	Questions	Reference Text	Answer
Week 2	How had Joshua been prepared to take on the role of leading God's people into the Promised land?	Numbers 11:28 Exodus 33:11 Numbers 27:18-23	
Week 2	How had Joshua demonstrated that he could be trusted for this very important role?	Exodus 17:8-14 Numbers 14:6-10 Numbers 14:28-30	
Week 2	How was Joshua assured that God wanted him to lead His people?	Joshua 1:1-9	

Godly Leadership

Leading Well, Chapters 3-24
Godly leaders have a vibrant relationship with the Lord, obey Him, and encourage His people. Use the table below to note how you see the following in each week of study (as applicable).

	What evidence do you see of Joshua's relationship with God?	Note specific ways Joshua was obedient to God.	How does Joshua encourage the faith of the people?
Week 3			
Week 4			
Week 5			
Week 6			
Week 7			
Week 8			
Week 9			

The Southern and Northern Campaigns Map

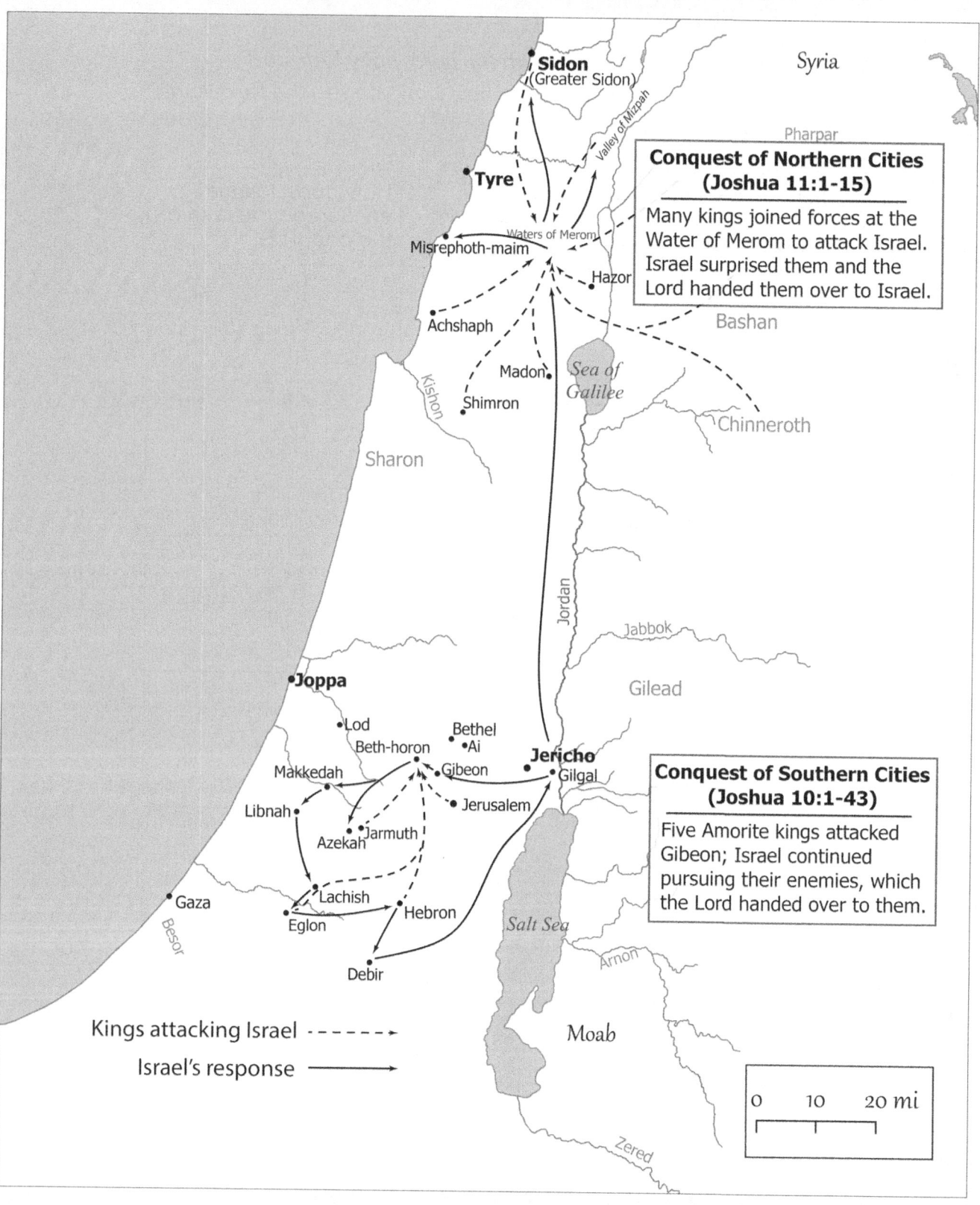

Conquest of Northern Cities (Joshua 11:1-15)

Many kings joined forces at the Water of Merom to attack Israel. Israel surprised them and the Lord handed them over to Israel.

Conquest of Southern Cities (Joshua 10:1-43)

Five Amorite kings attacked Gibeon; Israel continued pursuing their enemies, which the Lord handed over to them.

Kings attacking Israel -------->
Israel's response ———>

Boundaries of the Twelve Tribes Map

Light gray shading approximates unconquered portions of land

Thank you for studying with Seek and Find!
You can find additional studies, resources and downloads at
www.SeekandFindStudies.com

Made in the USA
Middletown, DE
08 November 2023